HONORING DR. WAYNE DYER

THE BOOK OF MENTORS

HONORING
DR. WAYNE DYER

CREATED BY MULTI #1
INTERNATIONAL BESTSELLING
AUTHOR & AWARD WINNING
SPEAKER ON HABITS

ERIK "MR AWESOME" SWANSON

HONORING DR. WAYNE DYER

THE BOOK OF
MENTORS

Keys To Success Honoring Legacy
Legends Zig Ziglar, Bob Proctor,
Dr. Wayne Dyer, & Jim Rohn

HONORING
WAYNE DYER

Hardback ISBN: 978-1-964330-03-7
Paperback ISBN: 978-1-964330-00-6

Celebrity Quotes

THE BOOK OF MENTORS

The Book of Mentors ~ Honoring Legacy Legends Zig Ziglar, Bob Proctor, Dr. Wayne Dyer, and Jim Rohn!

"Bravo, Bravo, Bravo! I want to compliment you in deciding to find a Mentor in your life. We all need them!"

Sir Bruno Serato ~ Philanthropist, Founder of Caterina's Club, CNN Man of the Year, Bestselling Author, Owner and Chef of the Anaheim White House ~ www.AnaheimWhitehouse.com

"A true mentor can offer you invaluable insights and advice that will help you navigate challenges and opportunities throughout your life."

Brian Tracy ~ Author, Speaker, Motivator ~ www.BrianTracy.com

"I changed directions, but I never changed the dream!"

Rudy Ruettiger ~ Author, Speaker, Inspirational Mentor, The Real Rudy from the movie 'RUDY' ~ www.RudyRuettiger.com

"Mentorship is life! Increase your world by learning from those who have stepped into greatness before you, and then strive to become a Mentor to those who follow you in your footsteps in the future."

Erik "Mr. Awesome" Swanson ~ Author, Speaker, Habits Coach ~ www.SpeakerErikSwanson.com

"There are two ways to learn. One is from the books we read and the other is being around smarter people. We become the average of the people we spend most of our time with People who do not read are no better off than people who cannot read to quote Mark Twain."

Don Green ~ President of the Napoleon Hill Foundation, Author, Speaker, Mentor ~ www.NapHill.org

"Be curious about your available sources of mentorship. There is often much to learn from those we perceive as less experienced."

Paul Blanchard ~ Author, Speaker, Habits Coach ~ www.WholeBodyMindset.com

"Success isn't the Gold Medal. It's the Silver Medal. The Gold Medal is significance. You achieve significance by helping someone else succeed. That is true mentorship!"

Ruben Gonzalez ~ Author, Speaker, Four-Time Olympian ~ www.TheLugeMan.com

"I have had some great mentors when I first started in the media business in NYC, that allowed me to take on some very tricky assignments at a very young age. Since then, I have been mentoring folks on a regular basis and it is incredibly satisfying to see them grow and succeed not only in business but also in their personal lives."

Larry Namer ~ Founder of E! Entertainment Television ~ www.EOnline.com

"Mentors are the teachers of life. 'If you give a man a fish, you feed him for a day. If you teach a man to fish, you feed him for a lifetime.' The mentors of life will perpetually become the heart and soul of progress and evolution in our world."

Jon Kovach Jr. ~ Author, Speaker, Mastermind Leader ~ www.SpeakerJonKovachJr.com

"Mentorship is a bridge between your VISION and its manifestation. It's having a Confidant by your side, who recognizes your greatness, and casts LIGHT on the path to accessing your Highest Self, and most elevated potential. Embracing the guidance of a mentor will INSPIRE and EMPOWER you to transform the ordinary into TRIUMPH. This sacred relationship evokes your BRILLIANCE, so you navigate through mists of uncertainty to the shores of CLARITY and ACHIEVEMENT."

Niurka ~ Transformation & Fulfillment Coach, NLP Master ~ www.NiurkaInc.com

"The gap between your divine potential and where you are today is called mentorship."

Darryll Stinson ~ Entrepreneur, Pastor, Speaker, Suicide Survivor ~ www.DarryllStinson.com

"A mentor is a great encourager. Mentorship is teaching from experience but deciding how to impart those lessons to others at the right times. Mentorship is all about experience that is shared with others. Then they encourage you to pursue the advice given."

Don Hobbs ~ Former President Success Magazine, Named Best Marketer by Tony Robbins, Co-Founder 7 Figure Coaching Secrets ~ www.DonHobbs.com

Global Speakers Mastermind &
Habitude Warrior Masterminds

Join us and become a member of our tribe! Our Global Speakers Mastermind is a virtual group of amazing thinkers and leaders who meet twice a month. Sessions are designed to be 'to the point' and focused while sharing fantastic techniques to grow your mindset as well as your pocketbooks. We also include famous guest speaker spots for our private Masterclasses. We also designate certain sessions for our members to mastermind with each other & and counsel on the topics discussed in our previous Masterclasses. It's time for you to join a tribe who truly cares about **YOU** and your future and start surrounding yourself with the famous leaders and mentors of our time. It is time for you to up-level your life, businesses, and relationships.

For more information to check out our Masterminds:
Team@HabitudeWarrior.com
www.DecideTobeAwesome.com

BECOME AN INTERNATIONAL
#1 BESTSELLING AUTHOR & SPEAKER

Habitude Warrior International has been highlighting award-winning Speakers and #1 Bestselling Authors for over 25 years. They know what it takes to become #1 in your field and how to get the best exposure around the world. If you have ever considered giving yourself the GIFT of becoming a well-known Speaker and a fantastically well known #1 Best-Selling Author, then you should email their team right away to find out more information in how you can become involved. They have the best of the best when it comes to resources in achieving the bestselling status in your particular field. Start surrounding yourself with the N.Y. Times Bestsellers of our time and start seeing your dreams become reality!

For more information to become a #1 Bestselling Author & Speaker on our Habitude Warrior Conferences
Please text the word AUTHORS to 619-304-6268
And also go to:
www.DecideToBeAwesome.com

HONORING DR. WAYNE DYER

Acknowledgement To Dr. Wayne Dyer

With immense respect and profound appreciation, I, along with the incredible team of authors in this series, extend our deepest gratitude to the revered Dr. Wayne Dyer. His extraordinary commitment and contributions have profoundly influenced countless lives worldwide. Dr. Wayne Dyer created a monumental legacy through his unparalleled mentorship and visionary leadership in personal and spiritual development.

We pay homage to his dedication and exceptional teachings, including his groundbreaking works such as *The Power of Intention* and *Your Erroneous Zones*, among many other transformative books, theories, and lectures. His wisdom and insights have inspired and influenced generations, reaching far beyond those who have drawn inspiration and empowerment from his teachings.

With the utmost respect, we sincerely thank Dr. Dyer from the bottom of our hearts for his enriched connections and relationships. May we all embody his teachings to elevate others and contribute to making this world an extraordinary place to live.

~ Erik "Mr. Awesome" Swanson ~ Multi #1 International Bestselling Author & Award-Winning Speaker

CONTENTS

Celebrity Quotes	The Book Of Mentors	7
Acknowledgement	To Dr. Wayne Dyer	13
Introduction	The Book Of Mentors	17
Honoring Dr. Wayne Dyer	A Tribute To A Legacy Legend Of Inspirations & Wisdom	21
Erik Swanson	How I Transformed My Life With The Wisdom Of Wayne	33
Rudy Ruettiger	You Must Have Character	43
Ruben Gonzalez	The Power Of Following The Leader	53
Don Green	Go The Extra Mile: The Keys Of Successful Mentors	65
Amy Keiderling	Embracing The Present Moment-Life Is Now	75
Dr. Angela Harden-Mack, MD	Manifest Your Greatness: A Journey To Fulfillment & Joy	79
Azadeh Bennett	The Power Of Choice	85
Dr. Betty Speaks	Confidence: The Key To Unleashing Your Full Potential	91
Bopi Villarino	The Transformative Power Of Mentorship	99
Daniel Kilburn	Life Is Now: Wayne Dyer Philosophy	105
Dawnese Openshaw	The Transformative Influence & Legacy Of Wayne Dyer	113
Donna Miner	You Get To Choose	121
Eileen E. Galbraith	Inspired To Greatness	131
Eric D. Jackson	Missed Mentorship: Nature & Its Principles Are A Good Mentor	137
Fred Moskowitz	Focus More On Enjoying Your Journey	145
Jeffrey Levine	Mentorship & The Power Of Purpose	151
Jon Kovach Jr.	The Law Of Divine Oneness	161

Julie Delgadillo	Self Mentorship & Reciprocal Empowerment	169
Kelli Hudson-Key	Mentorship In A Changing World	177
Lauren Cobb	Mentorship Of The Mind	187
Liz Sears	Beware Of The False Dichotomy	195
M. A. Fults	Another Stone For The Path	201
Maris Segal & Ken Ashby	A Grounding Legacy—Quotes To Live By	207
Mel Carr	The Power Of Intention & Presence In Business	215
Dr. Onika Shirley	Manifesting Your Potential	225
Ritu Chopra	The Triad Of Leadership	231
Sally Wurr	Not Everyone Can Be A Mentor-Choose Wisely	239
Sarah Lee	You Are Perfect Just The Way You Are	245
Stacey Hall	A Mentor's Path: Faith, Leadership, & Positivity	255
Steph Shinabery	Mentorship In An Evolving World	261
Taylor L. Cole	What's Weighing Down Your Mentorship Journey?	269
Vikki Rood	The Gift Of Giving Back	277
William Blake	Real Leadership—Real Impact	285

HONORING DR. WAYNE DYER

Introduction

THE BOOK OF MENTORS

Welcome to *The Book of Mentors* book series—an extraordinary journey of transformation, guidance, and wisdom. In the pages that follow, you will find a riveting exploration of mentorship, leadership, and the indelible impact of some of the most legendary figures in the realm of personal and professional development. This series is a meticulously curated anthology that pays homage to Zig Ziglar, Bob Proctor, Dr. Wayne Dyer, and Jim Rohn—four individuals whose lives and teachings have left an indelible mark on the world.

Mentorship is a timeless concept, a sacred exchange of wisdom, and a guiding light that has illuminated the paths of countless individuals seeking direction, clarity, and purpose. In today's fast-paced and ever-evolving world, the need for authentic leaders and mentors has never been greater. *The Book of Mentors* series emerges as a crucial resource, a compass for those in pursuit of excellence, wisdom, and a life lived in alignment with their highest values.

The celebrity authors, accompanied by the founder and creator, Erik "Mr. Awesome" Swanson and the contributing co-authors in this distinguished series, are an elite assembly of thinkers, leaders, and change-makers. Together, they are creating an everlasting resource of wisdom, intertwining together the legacy of Legacy Legends with the contemporary insights and experiences of today's thought leaders. Their voice, stories, and wisdom are integral roles and lessons as we collectively honor the mentors who have paved the way for us all.

Volume One: Honoring Legacy Legend Zig Ziglar

Zig Ziglar was a master of motivation, a beacon of integrity, and a true champion of the human spirit. His teachings transcended the boundaries of sales and business, touching the hearts and minds of individuals from all walks of life. In the first volume of *The Book of Mentors*, we celebrate Zig's unparalleled ability to inspire action, ignite passion, and instill a deep-seated belief in the potential that resides within each of us. We delve into the core principles that defined Zig's legacy, exploring how his teachings continue to guide, motivate, and transform lives today.

Volume Two: Honoring Legacy Legend Bob Proctor

Bob Proctor was a luminary in the world of personal development, a sage who unraveled the mysteries of the human mind and unlocked the secrets to limitless potential. His teachings on the law of attraction, the power of thought, and the transformative potential of belief have left an indelible mark on the world. In this second volume, we pay tribute to Bob's profound wisdom, delving into the principles that fueled his teachings and exploring the ripple effects of his mentorship across the globe. You will discover a wealth of knowledge, inspiration, and transformation.

Volume Three: Honoring Legacy Legend Dr. Wayne Dyer

Dr. Wayne Dyer was a spiritual guide, a philosopher, and a beacon of light in the journey of self-discovery and spiritual awakening. His teachings on intention, the power of thought, and the connection between the spiritual and the material world have transformed the lives of millions. In this third volume, we honor Wayne's legacy, exploring the depth of his wisdom and the profound impact of his teachings on the world. Just like the *Gifts from Eykis*, here you'll find a sanctuary of wisdom, guiding readers on a journey of inner-exploration, self-realization, and transformative growth.

Volume Four: Honoring Legacy Legend Jim Rohn

Jim Rohn was a philosopher, a mentor, and a visionary in the world of personal development. His teachings on the art of living, the power of personal responsibility, and the importance of continuous learning have shaped the course of mentorship across the globe. In this final volume, we celebrate Jim's timeless wisdom, delving into the principles and practices that defined his teachings. We paint a portrait of a man whose legacy continues to inspire, educate, and elevate the lives of individuals around the world.

The Book of Mentors book series is more than just a collection of books —it is a movement, a legacy, and a testament to the transformative power of mentorship. We are creating a legacy resource that speaks to the heart of what it means to be a mentor, a leader, and a guide in this ever-changing world.

As you turn the pages of each volume, we invite you to immerse yourself in the teachings, the stories, and the wisdom that have shaped the lives of millions. This series is a call to action—a reminder that the journey of mentorship is a lifelong pursuit, a sacred exchange, and a path to transformation. Together, we honor the Legacy Legends, celebrate the mentors who have guided us, and pave the way for the next generation of leaders and changemakers.

The journey begins here, and the path ahead is rich with possibility.

HONORING DR. WAYNE DYER

Honoring Dr. Wayne Dyer

A TRIBUTE TO A LEGACY LEGEND OF INSPIRATION & WISDOM

Few names resonate as profoundly as Dr. Wayne Dyer's in personal growth and transformation. A pioneering force in the self-development movement, Dr. Dyer's life's work stands to the deep principles of the power of human potential and the impact of a mind aligned with purpose. His teachings have inspired millions to reach beyond the ordinary and embrace the extraordinary within themselves. This third volume in *The Book of Mentors* book series, created by Erik "Mr. Awesome" Swanson and Integrity Publishing, is dedicated to honoring Dr. Wayne Dyer, a true legacy legend whose influence continues to uplift and inspire individuals across the globe.

A Tribute to a Legacy Legend: Dr. Wayne Dyer

Dr. Wayne Dyer was not just a prolific author or a charismatic speaker; he was a spiritual guide whose profound understanding of human nature helped countless individuals unlock the keys to living a fulfilled and meaningful life. His teachings, deeply rooted in the principles of self-reliance, personal responsibility, and the law of attraction, have left a lasting mark on personal development. Through his books, lectures, and media appearances, Dr. Dyer encouraged people to tap into their inner wisdom, transforming their lives through the power of thought and intention.

Early Life & Turning Point

Born on May 10, 1940, in Detroit, Michigan, Wayne Walter Dyer's early life was shaped by hardship and adversity. Growing up in foster homes after his father abandoned the family, young Wayne faced numerous challenges that could have easily led him down a path of despair. However, these early experiences only strengthened his resolve and became the bedrock of his teachings on self-reliance and resilience. The turning point in Dr. Dyer's life came when he was introduced to the works of Abraham Maslow and Viktor Frankl, which ignited his passion for psychology and self-improvement. This passion eventually led him to earn a doctorate in counseling psychology and set the stage for his future career as a transformational leader.

Philosophical Foundations & Key Teachings

At the core of Dr. Dyer's teachings is the belief that we are all capable of manifesting our desires through the power of intention. His philosophy was a blend of spiritual wisdom and practical psychology, emphasizing the importance of aligning one's thoughts, beliefs, and actions with one's highest purpose. In his groundbreaking book, *The Power of Intention*, Dr. Dyer explored how individuals could harness the energy of intention to create the life they desire. He taught that by changing our thoughts, we could change our reality—a principle that became a cornerstone of his work.

Dr. Dyer also drew heavily on Eastern philosophies, incorporating concepts such as mindfulness, meditation, and the Tao into his teachings. His book, *Change Your Thoughts, Change Your Life: Living the Wisdom of the Tao*, is a profound exploration of the Tao Te Ching, offering readers practical insights on how to apply ancient wisdom to modern life. His teachings encouraged individuals to embrace the flow of life, let go of ego-driven desires, and cultivate a deep sense of inner peace and contentment.

Significant Contributions & Career Highlights

Dr. Wayne Dyer's career was marked by numerous contributions that have impacted the world of self-help and personal development. His first major work, *Your Erroneous Zones* (1976), became one of the bestselling books of all time, with over 35 million copies sold worldwide. This book challenged conventional beliefs about self-esteem and personal responsibility, offering readers practical advice on overcoming negative thinking patterns and living a more fulfilling life.

Dr. Dyer authored over 40 books throughout his career, many of which became bestsellers. He was a regular presence on public television, where his specials attracted millions of viewers and became some of the most popular programming in PBS's history. His influence extended beyond his books and television appearances; he was also a sought-after speaker who inspired audiences around the world with his powerful messages of hope, love, and self-empowerment.

Personal Stories & Leadership

Dr. Dyer's journey was as inspirational as his teachings. He often shared stories from his own life, using them as powerful illustrations of the principles he taught. One of the most poignant stories he shared was his decision to forgive his father, who had abandoned him as a child. This act of forgiveness, described in his book, *I Can See Clearly Now*, was a turning point in his life, freeing him from years of resentment and allowing him to move forward with a heart full of love and compassion.

As a leader, Dr. Dyer was known for his humility and authenticity. He led not by dictating but by embodying the principles he espoused. His leadership was characterized by a deep commitment to helping others realize their full potential, and he did so with a generosity of spirit that touched the lives of everyone he encountered.

Mentorship & Impact on Others

Dr. Wayne Dyer mentored millions, both directly through his personal interactions and indirectly through his books, lectures, and media appearances. He had a unique ability to connect with people from all walks of life, offering them guidance and support as they navigated their paths of personal growth. His impact on others was profound and far-reaching, with many of today's leading self-help experts citing Dr. Dyer as a major influence in their own work.

One of the hallmarks of Dr. Dyer's mentorship was his emphasis on the importance of living authentically and being true to oneself. He encouraged his followers to listen to their inner voice, trust their intuition, and pursue their passions with unwavering determination. His teachings on the power of intention and the law of attraction have helped countless individuals manifest their dreams and create lives of abundance and joy.

Legacy & Continuing Influence

Dr. Wayne Dyer's legacy is one of empowerment, inspiration, and transformation. His teachings continue to resonate with new generations of seekers, offering them timeless wisdom on how to live meaningful, fulfilling lives. The principles he taught—such as the power of positive thinking, the importance of self-reliance, and the transformative power of love—remain as relevant today as they were when he first shared them.

The continued popularity of his books and the enduring impact of his teachings are evidence of his profound influence on the world. His work has not only transformed the lives of individuals but has also contributed to a broader cultural shift toward greater self-awareness, spiritual growth, and personal empowerment.

Foundational Principles & Truths

At the heart of Dr. Dyer's teachings were several foundational principles that he believed were essential for living a successful and fulfilling life. These principles include:

1. The Power of Intention: Dr. Dyer taught that our intentions shape our reality. By aligning our thoughts and actions with our highest purpose, we can manifest our desires and create a life of abundance and joy.

2. Self-Reliance: He emphasized the importance of taking personal responsibility for one's life. He believed that each individual has the power to shape their destiny and that true freedom comes from relying on oneself rather than external circumstances.

3. The Law of Attraction: Dr. Dyer strongly advocated the law of attraction, which posits that like attracts like. He taught us that focusing on positive thoughts and emotions can attract positive experiences into our lives.

4. The Importance of Forgiveness: Forgiveness was a central theme in Dr. Dyer's work. He believed that holding onto anger and resentment only harms the individual and that forgiveness is the key to healing and personal growth.

5. Living in the Present Moment: Dr. Dyer encouraged his followers to let go of past regrets and future anxieties and to live fully in the present moment. He believed that the present moment is the only place to find true happiness and fulfillment.

A Literary Legacy: Books That Transformed Lives

Dr. Wayne Dyer's literary contributions have left an enduring legacy in personal development. Some of his most influential works include:

Your Erroneous Zones: This groundbreaking book challenged readers to take control of their lives by identifying and overcoming negative thinking patterns. It remains one of the bestselling self-help books of all time.

The Power of Intention: In this book, Dr. Dyer explored how the power of intention can be harnessed to create the life we desire. He provided practical advice on aligning our thoughts, beliefs, and actions with our highest purpose.

Change Your Thoughts, Change Your Life: This book offers a deep exploration of the Tao Te Ching, providing readers with insights on how to apply ancient wisdom to modern life.

Excuses Begone!: In this book, Dr. Dyer challenges readers to let go of the excuses holding them back and embrace their true potential.

I Can See Clearly Now: This memoir offers a retrospective of Dr. Dyer's life, sharing the lessons and insights he gained along his journey.

Philosophy & Self-Image

Dr. Dyer placed great emphasis on the role of self-image in determining one's success and fulfillment in life. He believed that how we see ourselves directly impacts what we can achieve. He taught us that we could overcome barriers and achieve unprecedented success by reshaping our self-image to reflect confidence, competence, and optimism.

Personal & Professional Development

Dr. Dyer was a staunch advocate for continuous learning and growth. He believed that personal development was the cornerstone of professional success and urged his followers to cultivate lifelong habits of self-improvement. His teachings on self-reliance, the power of intention, and the importance of living authentically have helped countless individuals achieve success in their personal and professional lives.

Goals & Success

For Dr. Wayne Dyer, pursuing goals was never solely about material success; it was deeply intertwined with personal growth, self-discovery, and realizing one's higher purpose. He believed that setting clear, intentional goals provided direction and focus in life, but the true essence of success lay in the journey rather than the destination.

Dr. Dyer often emphasized that goals should be aligned with one's inner values and true desires rather than being dictated by societal expectations or external pressures. He taught that success comes from living authentically and striving to fulfill one's potential in all areas of life—spiritual, emotional, intellectual, and physical.

His approach to goal setting was holistic. He encouraged individuals to set goals that contributed to their personal well-being and the greater good. He believed that when goals are rooted in love, service, and the desire to make a positive impact, they become a powerful force for transformation.

Mentorship & Beliefs

Mentorship was a key theme in Dr. Dyer's life and work. He viewed himself not just as a teacher but as a guide, helping others navigate their own paths of self-discovery and personal development. Dr. Dyer's mentorship extended beyond formal settings—through his books, lectures, and media appearances, he mentored millions of individuals around the world.

Dr. Dyer believed that mentorship was about more than imparting knowledge; it was about empowering others to recognize and embrace their own potential. He encouraged those he mentored to trust in their inner wisdom, question limiting beliefs, and cultivate a mindset of abundance and possibility.

A cornerstone of his belief system was the idea that everyone has the capacity for greatness and that anyone can achieve their dreams with the right mindset and guidance. He often spoke about the importance of surrounding oneself with positive influences and seeking mentors who inspire and challenge us to grow.

A Legacy of Empowerment & Excellence

Dr. Wayne Dyer's legacy is one of profound empowerment and excellence. Throughout his life, he remained committed to helping others unlock their potential and live their highest truth. His teachings have empowered countless individuals to overcome obstacles, surpass limiting beliefs, and create lives of purpose and fulfillment.

His legacy is carried forward by those who continue to be inspired by his work—individuals who have embraced his teachings and used them to transform their own lives and the lives of others. The impact of his work is evident in the many testimonials, stories, and tributes from those his wisdom has touched.

Dr. Dyer's dedication to excellence was evident in everything he did. Whether writing a book, delivering a lecture, or mentoring an individual, he approached every endeavor with a deep purpose and a commitment to making a positive impact. This commitment to excellence has ensured that his work continues to resonate and inspire long after his passing.

The Timeless Principles of Success

Dr. Wayne Dyer's principles are timeless, outperforming the changes and challenges of the modern world. His teachings on the power of intention, the importance of self-reliance, and the law of attraction remain as relevant today as they were when he first addressed them.

Dr. Dyer's success principles are universal and applicable to anyone, regardless of their background, circumstances, or aspirations. His teachings provide a roadmap for personal and professional growth, offering practical guidance on how to align one's thoughts, beliefs, and actions with one's highest goals.

One of the most enduring aspects of Dr. Dyer's work is his ability to distill complex spiritual and psychological concepts into accessible, actionable advice. This has allowed his teachings to reach a broad audience and has ensured that his wisdom will continue to guide future generations.

Celebrating a Life Well Lived

Dr. Wayne Dyer passed away on August 29, 2015, perpetuating a legacy that inspires and uplifts countless individuals worldwide. His life exemplified the power of intention, the importance of living authentically, and the transformative potential of love and compassion.

As we reflect on Dr. Dyer's contributions, we celebrate not just the vast body of work he left behind but the profound impact he had on the lives of those who had the privilege of learning from him. His teachings continue to offer guidance, inspiration, and hope to those seeking to live their best lives.

Dr. Wayne Dyer's life was one of purpose, passion, and profound wisdom. He dedicated himself to helping others realize their potential, and in doing so, he created a legacy that will endure for generations to come. As we honor his memory, we are reminded of the power of a life lived with intention, integrity, and love—a life that continues to shine as a beacon of hope and inspiration for all.

~ Habitude Warrior Team ~

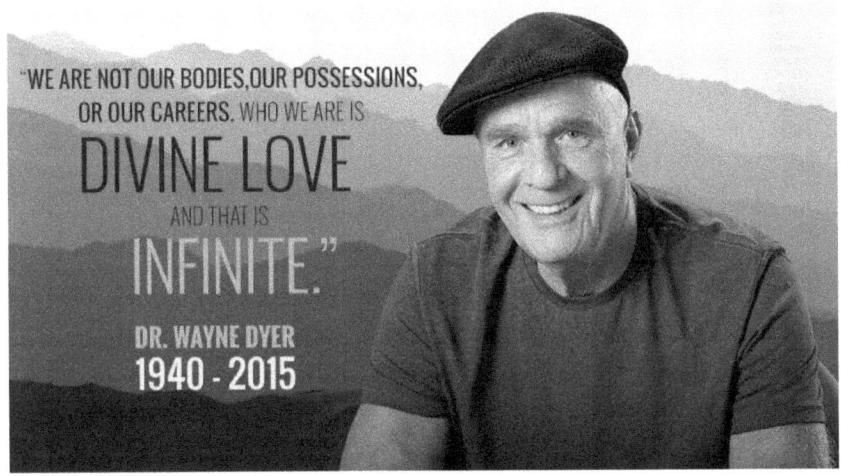

ERIK SWANSON

HOW I TRANSFORMED MY LIFE WITH THE WISDOM OF WAYNE

"When you squeeze an orange, orange juice comes out, because that's what's inside. When you are squeezed, what comes out is what is inside."
~ **Dr. Wayne Dyer**

I started my self-development journey when I was in my teens. A good friend of mine handed me a book when I was 19 years old. The book was titled, *Your Erroneous Zones*, by Wayne Dyer. At the time, I had no idea I needed Dr. Wayne Dyer as much as I did. Looking back now, I can honestly say that I transformed my life with the wisdom of Wayne!

Timing is Always Divine

What I have noticed in my life is that timing is always perfect and Divine. It may not seem that way at the moment, but in hindsight, it's so noticeable. You see, I was going through the biggest breakup of my life and the world basically stopped for me. Ha, looking back at it, it was simply my puppy love relationship I was currently in with my girlfriend who was about to move out of state to attend her freshman year at her university. We made the decision that it would be better to break things off so that we could both focus on our studies. This devastated me at the time.

My friend saw how depressed I was and offered the book to me to read. Wow, it put things into perspective in such a way that it brought me out of my depression and allowed me to realize that I was and am truly in charge of my own thoughts and feelings. Hi Danielle, if you're reading this.

Our Thoughts are Truly Ours

This concept was first taught to me by Wayne Dyer. He taught me that we can choose the way we talk to ourselves. We can choose the way we word sentence patterns to reflect a better outcome. It's an inner game if you really think about it.

You see, I used to blame others for the way I was feeling. I used to make excuses and justify why certain things were happening to me. I used to talk to myself in such a negative way that simply didn't serve me. All it did was mistakenly convince me that I was not in charge and things were happening 'to' me.

Then, I realized, after diving deep into the work by Dr. Dyer, that I truly am in charge of my own thoughts and actions. My feelings were directly attached to my thoughts and I quickly realized that if I wanted to feel differently, I simply had to think differently.

Was it easy to do? Of course not, at least not at first. It takes practice. Like any other habit, it takes practice and consistency to incorporate a new habit into our lives. But, it's worth it!

Time to Take Action

At some point in our lives, we need to make that decision to cut out our bad habits that simply are not serving us, and incorporate new, positive habits. This is exactly what I did. I felt like I was hitting rock bottom with my breakup, and I had to pick up the pieces and start thinking differently and changing my habits daily to be able to achieve that higher ground I was looking for.

I started to notice that all of the teachings I learned from Dr. Dyer and his books that I devoured not only had an impact on how I was dealing with my breakup at the time, but I noticed it assisted me in every single relationship, including with my friends, my father, and even strangers I would meet. This was amazing to me. I felt like I had a new magic power. It started to become a game to me in which I would welcome challenging situations so that I could see which technique I would use to make the situation an amazing one with a positive outcome for everyone involved.

Make it a Game

I would highly recommend making these positive experiences and techniques into a game you play with yourself. No one needs to know you are practicing these new and improved magical techniques of relationship building. See how many interactions you can change into positive ones. Start keeping track of your successes in these areas. You will start to realize that each time you revert to your old ways of thinking or blaming or casting excuses, you may receive the old negative outcomes. But, if you start keeping track of your new success quotient, you will start to realize this new thinking pattern truly works. The world is now your oyster!

Magical Techniques

Here are some magical techniques and teachings I picked up by Dr. Dyer and added in my own personality to them. I'm happy to share them with you as well. Give these a try and watch your relationships grow to amazing, new heights.

1. Become a master at listening. Listening skills are so vitally important to not only show that you value the person you are speaking to, but you also value their input. I can't tell you how much this technique alone has increased the value of my relationships in my life. Quick hint: even if you are not totally interested in what the other person is saying, act as if you are. You will soon become the person known to others as a great listener, and, honestly, people typically are not

35

looking for you to provide the answers for everything. They simply want to be heard.

2. Create a habit of making great eye contact with everyone you come in contact with. This technique does so many things that have positive outcomes. The first thing it does is that it shows respect to the other person. It consciously and also unconsciously makes the person feel like they are the only thing in the world you are currently focused on. This is huge in relationship building. Having great eye contact also allows you to see different facial expressions the other individual may have. A huge percentage of communication comes from non-verbal cues. Use this to your advantage in building that relationship. Eye contact also builds confidence and trust. It shows that you believe in yourself and you believe in them as well.

3. Do not interrupt! Make a habit of holding back from interrupting and hold your comments that you would like to share for when there's a break in the conversation. This gives honor to the other individual and will subconsciously stick in their minds that you truly are respectful and honor them for what they are saying.

4. Repeat and clarify. Another great habit I use is the habit of repeating back to them what you just heard. This does two major things. The first thing it does is communicate to the other person that you truly are not only listening to them, but also understanding what they are trying to get across to you in the conversation. The second thing that's really cool is if you clarify what they said to you by rephrasing their sentence back to them. This will allow the conversation to continue and most of them time they will reply by saying the word 'yes,' and continuing with their sentence. *Advanced Technique: Any time you can get them to say the word 'yes' back to you is awesome! This literally means that they are agreeing with you and it sticks in their mind that you are the type of person they agree with most, if not all of the time.

5. Compliment them. Get in the habit of finding something to compliment someone on. I personally look for something to compliment someone on in every single conversation. It's very

important to make sure you are genuine in your compliment. There's always something you can compliment someone on. For example, you can compliment someone on their glasses or their zoom background, or ask them if they have been working out because they look amazing!

Mentors are All Around Us

Mentors can be found if you are open to them. Clearly, Dr. Wayne Dyer was one of my first mentors in my self-development area of my life. I had a goal way back in my life that I would love to meet the one and only Wayne Dyer someday.

Fast forward about 10 years from the first time I read one of Wayne's books. I was working with my mentor, Brian Tracy, who took me under his wing to teach me the business of speaking and coaching. We had an event I was scheduling for one of my companies in which Brian Tracy couldn't actually make that specific event. I asked Brian if he had any suggestions as to whom we should seek out to speak at this particular event of ours. Brian suggested I reach out to Dr. Wayne Dyer, and even gave me a contact number to see if I could connect with Wayne.

I was so excited and nervous all at the same time to call Wayne's office. But, after a few pep talks to myself, there I was, dialing the number Brian had just given me. I called. The phone was ringing. My hands and palms were sweaty. I could tell that my breathing was very rapid. I was so nervous! This was the office of the person I had learned all of the amazing techniques from his teachings and books over many, many years. Of course I'm going to be very nervous. But, there I was, dialing the number anyway. What could go wrong, right?

After three rings, the phone answered. The voice that picked up was an extremely familiar voice to me. The voice I so distinctively knew said, "Hello, this is Wayne. May I help you?" WOW, I literally had Wayne Dyer on the phone with me! I couldn't believe it. It was really him! I could not believe that Brian Tracy had given me the direct cell number for Dr. Wayne Dyer. I was so excited, but my excitement quickly turned to fear. I freaked out and didn't know what to say. There was dead space on my end of the phone because no words were coming out of my mouth. I did the only thing I could think of at the time—I hung up! Oh my God, I just hung up the phone on Dr. Wayne Dyer! Yes, you heard me right.

I was so floored by my actions and embarrassed that I didn't know what to do. Can you imagine Wayne on the other end of the phone wondering why someone is hanging up on him?

So, after a few minutes, I picked up my dignity and redialed his number. He answered again and I pretended like nothing happened. We had a great talk and proceeded to chat about speaking at one of my events.

To this day, I have never really shared this story with anyone except for my dear friend, Dr. Denis Waitley. Denis and I were chatting about some of the most embarrassing moments in our self-development careers, and somehow, this story came out of me. I never had the heart to let Wayne know what happened that day and I had the absolute amazing pleasure of meeting Wayne a few times over the following years before his passing.

Fast forward another five years or so, and I was at another one of my Habitude Warrior and Speaker Hearts events in which we had an amazing speaker who had such an incredible story of triumph. She knew I was a huge fan of Dr. Dyer's, so she decided to actually wear one of Wayne's purple beret hats to our event and allowed me to wear it for part of the day. This was Dr. Wayne Dyer's actual beret. Wow. It still gives me chills thinking about it, him, and all of the relationship-building techniques I truly learned from one of my mentors.

We love you, Wayne! Thank you!

ERIK SWANSON

As an Award-Winning International Keynote Speaker and Multi-Time #1 International Bestselling Author, Erik "Mr. Awesome" Swanson is in great demand around the world! He speaks to an average of more than one million people per year. Mr. Swanson has the honor to have been invited to speak to many schools around the world including the prestigious Harvard University. He is also a recurring Faculty Member of CEO Space International as well as an Alumni Keynoter at Vistage Executive Coaching. Mr. Swanson is also the recipient of 2024's International Book Impact Award and the United States Presidential Lifetime Achievement Award presented by the White House in 2024 for his ongoing community service and philanthropy work. Erik's speeches can be found on Amazon Prime TV as well as joining the Ted Talk Family with his latest speech called, "A Dose of Awesome."

Erik got his start in the self-development world by mentoring directly under Brian Tracy. Quickly climbing to become the top trainer around the world from a group of over 250 handpicked coaches, Erik started to surround himself with the best of the best and very quickly started to be invited to speak on stages alongside such greats as Jim Rohn, Bob Proctor, Les Brown, Sharon Lechter, Jack Canfield, Lisa Nichols, and Joe Dispenza—just to name a few. Erik has created and developed the super-popular Habitude Warrior Conferences and Speaker Hearts Mastermind & Retreats, which have a two-year waiting list and include 33 top-named speakers from around the world. They are 'Ted Talk' style events which have quickly climbed to the top 10 events not to miss in the United States! He is the creator, founder, and CEO of the Habitude Warrior Mastermind, Global Speakers Mastermind, and Cafe Mastermind. He is also the creator and publisher of many book series such as *The 13 Steps To Riches* book series as well as *The Principles of David & Goliath* book series. His motto is clear: "NDSO!": No Drama – Serve Others!

www.SpeakerErikSwanson.com

HONORING DR. WAYNE DYER

RUDY RUETTIGER

YOU MUST HAVE CHARACTER

Character is the answer! The right mentor for anyone is someone with character. You need mentors with character—subsequently, you need to strengthen your character if you are to become a mentor to others.

For those seeking mentors, you should focus on looking for people who have the attributes of a person with great character. That doesn't mean you are looking for characters in the humorous sense. You are looking for people with a great mindset, attitude, and disposition.

The Main Attributes of Someone with Character

First, seek people who do what they say they will do. Second, if they do what they say, they must also back what they say. People of character make decisions and stick to their choices, even if they make mistakes, but they usually bounce back and do the right thing. You must know that not everybody is perfect, and you, too, shouldn't plan to be perfect—you're not perfect, and that's okay.

You will have to jump out of your way and take risks throughout your decisions in life. You've got this—be bold. Be brave. Have courage. Build character. Don't be afraid to fail. Eliminate doubt. You can eliminate any doubts by not having doubting friends around you. Then, all of a sudden, you become a mentor without saying, "I'm a mentor." Talk is cheap. Work is real. Action is real. That's how you become a mentor.

43

Character Trumps Perfectionism

There are many wealthy perfectionists, but you want to avoid going to dinner with them.

While I was speaking at Notre Dame, I saw a young boy and his mother sitting in the restaurant where I was staying. I could tell that he was struggling with something. He had a Notre Dame boxing team hat on. I also boxed at Notre Dame, so I wanted to see what was happening because they looked a little stressed out.

So, I went over and said, "Hey, I boxed."

He says, "Well, I did box." The mother interrupted and said, "Yeah, he sure did. But he was just relieved from Notre Dame because he failed out of school."

"Wow," I said, "Man, can I have a seat? So, how'd you fail out, man?"

He said, "Well, it's a long story."

The mother again interjected and said, "Tommy had perfect SATs." She continued, "And Tommy was a captain of his hockey team. He was valedictorian. He had perfect grades. But after COVID hit, they locked him in a room for eighteen days. He has ADHD and went absolutely nuts and gave up on his schoolwork. He needed good friends with character but had the wrong friends around him at the time."

I answered, "Oh, that's an easy fix. You can go back to Notre Dame."

The mom reluctantly said, "No, they said he's done!"

I argued back, "That's what they said, yes. But that's what 'they' said, right, Tommy? That's not what Tommy said, though. Do you want to go back, Tommy?"

Tommy said, "Yeah, of course I do!"

I answered, "Okay, Tommy. You are going to go back and ask them what you have to do to get back in." I asked more clarification questions, "Where do you live, Tommy?"

He answered, "Long Island, New York."

I said, "Oh good. I could help you out there. I have a friend at Long Island University. I'm going to call him because he's the university's Athletic Director. You're going to go intern for him. Would you do that? You are not going to get paid? But would you do it?"

He, of course, said, "Yes."

I continued, "While you intern for him, you will need to take the courses you need to do there to pass, and then you'll be back in at Notre Dame, once you pass the courses you need. Would you do that?"

He said, "Of course."

I continued, "But here's the real hard one. All of that I mentioned is the easy part. Can you make a bed every day?"

And he looked at me and said, "What do you mean?"

"Can you make your bed every day?" I pressed harder, "And you clean your room? Before you do everything I suggested, you'll be back here at Notre Dame if you do those small tasks before anything else. Your character will develop, and they'll have no trouble accepting you back after all that has happened."

We shook hands, and now, he's made it back to Notre Dame boxing again. He recently won the Bingo Bounce boxing event. The moral in this story isn't that he made it back into the school but that his character developed while he pursued his goals. Your character will always help you arrive at your goals. Plus, they (Notre Dame) will respect you for what you did, and they will listen because it's not about what you say; it's what you do. That's character. That's the kind of character you should seek in a mentor.

Too many people talk and talk and speak awful, disingenuous crap. They self-proclaim themselves as a "mentor" because they made money doing something, but they severely lack character. It's taking action (doing what you say) to back up the talk.

If Rudy were in Webster's Dictionary, the definition would say "action" and "persistence." You've got to push through the tough times. You must have persistence and persevere.

Jonathan Favreau was one the best directors and filmmakers in Hollywood. His comment was, "I'm a Rudy. I pushed through things when times got hard. Not that I always make the right choices, but you got to push through, forget what you did wrong, and move forward and do the right things."

Those principles and statements make sense to me because that's what it's all about. Too many people bear this narcissistic attitude of who we think we are, which we are not. I have made that mistake, as we all do at times. It's okay to make mistakes because, again, be impeccable with your words, and back your words with action. That's being and having character.

What's the first thing we should do if we feel beaten up or down on our luck?

If you don't have spirituality, you don't have much. You are a child of God—it's not a religious thing. If you turn to and think religion is your answer, you're wrong. Too many people fall for manipulating religious beliefs when there's only one belief you should consider. That simple belief should be in God. That's it. There is no other answer, in my opinion and experience.

Although it is in my character to play at the level of gameplay at every single opportunity given, I have only given up on one thing in his life. I've given up on the bullshit. Consequently, I give up on the people who will plant doubt and fear and on those who cultivate a belief and structure of fear. But I will never give up on what I believe in and what is right, and neither should you.

You may be reading this and asking yourself, "How do I know what's right?" What's right comes from inside you—it's your intuition. I know that God gives me the way and points me to what's right and wrong. Also, if you have the right people around you with character, courage, and commitment, you will make the right choices and choose the right things. Not everybody needs to be rich. Not everybody needs to have abundance. You are already abundant through knowledge, wisdom, and character. You've already got all that. Some of the poorest people give the best advice compared to the richest people.

How do people build that muscle for knowledge, wisdom, and character?

Faith is your greatest source of intuition. With faith, you will not be afraid to die. If you've developed a fear of death, you've lost your faith's personal touch. Too many people stop short of reaching their goals and dreams because they have stopped trusting their beliefs and faith.

My parents taught me what not to do in life. I'm not going to do what they did. That's like a coach. I'm not saying my parents were terrible, but they made mistakes and made significant progress for us. What they did wrong is what I won't replicate and repeat. My dad said, "Don't do what I did. Learn from what I did wrong."

Just like identifying a mentor with character, you can recognize the difference between a good and bad coach. The first thing a bad coach does is they'll start blaming you. They'll make you feel bad about what you did. A good coach reassures you. They'll iterate, "We'll get it next time. Don't worry about it. You wouldn't be out there unless I didn't believe in you." A good coach has character and recognizes we all make mistakes, which is part of the game.

Dave Scatchard is a retired professional hockey player who played in the National Hockey League (NHL) with the Vancouver Canucks, New York Islanders, Boston Bruins, Phoenix Coyotes, Nashville Predators, and St. Louis Blues. The Vancouver Canucks selected him 42nd overall in the 1994 NHL Entry Draft. He had a roller-coaster career, playing fourteen years in the NHL. He wrote in a signed copy of his book to me, "To

Rudy, thank you for being such an inspiration to my life. Let's make this book something better. You're my hero." That's a mentor.

Kobe Bryant said, "Rudy's my hero." Any regular guy says, "Let's get a mentor." Kobe was not going to mentor you. Kobe would kick your ass if you don't do what's right or work hard enough to win. Kobe would push you to the next level.

Is there always a next level?

Your next level is what you want. You better push yourself to be that. My mentor, besides God Himself, is between me and the one I look up to. My heroes and mentors always push me to the next level.

Tommy's mother wrote me recently, saying, "Now I'm dealing with my other son, a freshman at Michigan. He wanted to get into the engineering program because it was his dream school. However, he's in a bad dormitory and doesn't have good-character friends. He was super social and popular in high school and wanted to get into a fraternity, but he recently found out he didn't. He hasn't met many friends while at school so far, and he's super lonely. So, I'm flying him home tomorrow to talk to him about transferring to Notre Dame. Whenever one of my kids is going through something, you are there for them."

I responded to her, "Michigan has no sense of community. It's too big of a school and very spread out. I would love to see him transfer to Notre Dame next year."

Every kid goes through a cultural change throughout their life. Some kids pick the culture because of the status or the big, recognized brand name. It would help if you chose a culture that feels right to you. In my case, I had no right to go to or be accepted into Notre Dame. But I thought I should be there.

If that's what you feel, you must fight for that. Once you fight for what you feel, you make it, and that's what this young boy didn't have. He needed to fight for what he wanted. With his brother Tommy, he had to fight to get back into Notre Dame and back on the boxing team. He still wanted to be at Notre Dame. This other young boy needed to go back to Michigan to see if he felt that same feeling that would lead him to fight for what he wanted. He needed to feel that he should go to Notre Dame or any other school and fight for what he wanted. He doesn't have to go to Michigan to be successful. People throughout the world need to understand that. The name and school will not make you successful. Your desire and drive to fight for what you want will.

Most leaders and mentors you interview won't give it to you straight. They say, "I can guarantee this and that…." To become a better leader, coach, mentor, or hero, you must always work hard, build character, and fight for what you want. There is no easy way to success and personal achievement.

"March on to victory."
~ Notre Dame Victory March

RUDY RUETTIGER

Against all odds on a gridiron in South Bend, Indiana, Daniel "Rudy" Ruettiger carved his name into history books as perhaps the most inspiring graduate of the University of Notre Dame. As fans cheered "RU-DY!, RU-DY!," (which is now considered to be the underdog chant of a lifetime) this "five-foot nothin', a hundred and nothin'... without a speck of athletic ability," sacked the quarterback in the last 27 seconds of the only play in the only game of his college football career. He is the first player in the school's history to be carried off the field on the shoulders of his teammates.

As the son of an oil refinery worker and third of 14 children, Rudy rose from valleys of discouragement and despair to the pinnacles of success. It took years of fierce determination to overcome obstacles and criticisms, yet Rudy achieved his first dream - to attend Notre Dame and play football for the Fighting Irish.

In 1993, TRISTAR Productions immortalized Rudy's life story with the blockbuster film, *RUDY*. Written and directed by Angelo Pizzo and David Anspaugh, the award-winning team who brought us *HOOSIERS*, the critically acclaimed *RUDY* received "Two Thumbs Up" from Siskel and Ebert, is considered one of the "Most Inspirational Movies of All Time" by Fandango, IMDB, Ranker and countless other websites. *USA TODAY* performed the films musical score, live in perfect time during a sold-out screening of the film.

Rudy's candid nature and willingness to connect with every person he meets with a bold, refreshing and relevant message has poised him to exemplify his message in his real life, over-coming obstacles, persevering through adversity and making every second count. He is a willing, able and inspirational speaker who is looking forward to being a part of your next event. Millions have been inspired by the movie *RUDY*, now let the man behind the movie inspire you!

He co-founded the RUDY FOUNDATION, whose mission is to strengthen communities by offering scholarships in education, sports, and the performing arts. The focus of the Rudy Foundation is to make a positive impact by bringing people together cognitively, emotionally, physically and spiritually.

The RUDY AWARDS™ is another program the Rudy Foundation developed to recognize children who make an outstanding, exceptional effort to do their personal best every day, overcome obstacles, set goals, stay on track to reach their dreams, and build the qualities of character, courage, and commitment in their lives. The RUDY AWARDS™ is about a child's heart, will to change, and desire for self-improvement. Rudy has two awesome children; Jessica Noel Ruettiger and Daniel Joseph Ruettiger.

www.RudyRuettiger.com

HONORING DR. WAYNE DYER

RUBEN GONZALEZ

THE POWER OF FOLLOWING THE LEADER

When I was growing up, my dad always said this to me: "If you have to cross a minefield, it makes sense to follow someone who's already crossed it."

He meant that you need to find someone who's already done what you want to do, and follow in their footsteps. Find a coach or mentor who's been in the trenches and has fruit on the trees—results. Following the leader is the fastest and easiest way to achieve any goal. Following the leader is the shortcut to success.

Whenever I share this in my keynote presentations, I always get pushback from my audiences.

Invariably, they say to me, "But those people are so busy. I wouldn't want to impose." So, I have to explain.

Have you ever heard people say that successful people are seldom fulfilled or satisfied? You know why that is? It's because success isn't the Gold Medal. Most people think it is, but it's not. It's the Silver Medal.

You know what the Gold Medal is? It's significance. You achieve significance by helping someone else succeed. You get it by creating a ripple effect of success. By making a difference in someone else's life. By making the world a better place. Significance is the Gold Medal.

As long as you're willing to wholeheartedly take action on whatever your mentor says you need to do to achieve your goal, you owe it to them to ask for help. Your mentor will help you get your Silver Medal, and you'll help them get their Gold Medal: making a difference.

Mentorship is a two-way street: the mentor's job is to teach, correct, and encourage; the mentee's job is to be a good follower and follow the mentor's advice by taking action immediately.

The same is true in the coach/athlete relationship. If both of you do your job, the team has a better chance to win.

Finding a coach or mentor who's already done what you want to do and asking them for help is only the first step. The next step is to follow their advice right away. Taking action is where the rubber meets the road.

For the longest time, I had trouble following my leaders' advice...

Olympic Dream

Ever since I was a little kid, I wanted to be in the Olympics, but I'm not a great athlete, so I didn't think it was possible, and I never pursued it.

Then, when I was twenty-one years old, I was watching the Olympics on TV, and I saw this little guy, who must have been five feet one and weighed 110 lbs, soaking wet. This kid won the Gold Medal in figure skating—Scott Hamilton.

When I saw Scott Hamilton, everything changed. I said to myself, "If THAT little guy can win, I can at least play. I'll be in the next Olympics. It's a done deal. I just have to find a sport." My strength was tenacity, so I started looking for sports that matched my strength. I chose the luge.

I lived in Houston, Texas. Hot, humid, flat, sticky Houston, Texas. I didn't know where the luge track was. So, I wrote Sports Illustrated, and I asked them, "Where do you go to learn how to luge?" They said, "Lake Placid, New York. That's where the track is."

So, I called Lake Placid. "I'm an athlete here in Houston, and I want to learn how to luge so I can be in the Olympics in four years. Will you help me?"

The guy asked, "How old are you?"

"Twenty-one."

He started laughing. "Twenty-one? Forget it, man. You're way too old! We start them off when they're 8-9-10 years old. By now, you should have ten years of experience. No way!"

I didn't know what to do. I only knew that hanging up the phone was NOT an option. That would have been the end of my dream. I just kept talking with him.

Finally, he said, "There's a beginner's camp coming up in a few weeks. Be there."

So, I went to Lake Placid.

I've always been very independent. That's a nice way of saying I don't like people telling me what to do. I like to be in control. Even so, before I went to Lake Placid, I promised myself that I would submit to my coaches' leadership. After all, who was I to question the Olympic coaches?

But it was so hard for me to follow their advice. And I paid the price. The first couple of years I broke my foot twice, my knee, my elbow, my hand, my thumb, and a couple of ribs. At first, I was crashing four out of five times. Four out of five! That hurt. But I kept at it. And after a while, I was crashing three out of five. Oh, that was a great day! Then one out of ten.

By the end of the second year, I was crashing one out of a hundred. I finally figured out how to drive that darned sled. Then I started competing internationally to try to be one of the fifty men who would compete in the Olympics.

I competed in the Calgary, Albertville and Salt Lake City Olympics. But it would have been so much easier if I'd followed my coach's advice right away.

The Problem

Olympic coaches and business leaders agree that very few people want to follow the leader anymore. That's a problem because it keeps them from being their best.

In the old days, if you wanted to master a craft, you became an apprentice. You found someone who was an expert, and you followed their advice.

What's the point of having a mentor or a coach if you don't follow their advice? If you want to be your best, you have to follow the leader.

Luge Run

People always ask me, "What's it feel like? What's it feel like to hurl yourself down an icy chute at 80-90 MPH? Is it scary?"

Yes, it's scary, especially for me because I started so late. Let me walk you through a luge run and show you how I resisted following my coach.

The luge track starts fifty stories up the mountain. Fifty stories! That's way up there. You're going to be sliding down the mountain on a little bitty sled that's just a piece of fiberglass on a couple of steel runners. You'll be hitting speeds of 80-90 MPH, and you have no brakes.

I know. This is not a normal sport.

You're up at the start. Your hands are sweaty, your mouth is dry, the hair is standing on the back of your neck. Because you know what could happen down there—broken bones, concussions, dislocations, and worse.

Coach gives you a pat on the back and moves away. You have spikes on your fingertips you'll use to pick up speed after the start. You test them on the ice. They feel good.

You take a couple of deep breaths to get yourself centered. Visor goes down, you grip the handles, and one, two, and you pull.

You paddle furiously to build up speed and you lay down. In no time, you're doing 50, 60, 70, 80 miles per hour. As the speed increases, so does the fear. You're focused on a spot thirty feet in front of you, just flying down the track.

You hit a curve and you're ten, fifteen feet up on the wall pulling up to six Gs. Six Gs! I weigh 200lbs. That's 1,200 pounds squashing you against the wall. It feels like a polar bear is sitting on your chest.

You see the exit and you drive down. You cross the finish line and how are you going to stop? You have no brakes. Well, you force yourself to sit up on the sled, and BOOM, you get thrown back with this 80 MPH wind. You pick up the front of the sled, you dig your heels in, and you slow down, slow down, slow down.

It takes two hundred yards to come to a stop. Two football fields! You get off your sled, and about five seconds later, the adrenaline rush hits you. The fear hits you like a sledgehammer.

"I'm never doing that again. I'm going back to soccer." I was a soccer player. "Soccer's soft, it's warm, you don't get killed in soccer. What was I thinking? Why did I do the luge? Why didn't I do ping-pong, or curling, or something like that?" And you want to quit with every fiber in your being.

Fortunately, there's a walkie-talkie down at the finish line. There's a bunch of walkie-talkies because there are coaches up and down the track. My coach is a four-time Olympian and a three-time world champion from Austria. He's the best of the best. He's the Michael Jordan of luge.

He's six-foot-six and looks like and sounds like Arnold Schwarzenegger. I pick up the walkie-talkie and I'm still out of breath. "Coach, this is Ruben."

"Ruben, nach, c'mon. You must point your toes more. And Ruben put your head further back. And Ruben, you were so late on curve six. You must steer harder, harder, harder on curve six. And Ruben, relax, relax. Be one with the sled. Have fun."

Click.

Have fun? How am I going to have fun when I'm scared half to death? Coach started when he was five years old, for Pete's sake. I think, "Coach is nuts. He's nuts... But he's right. All my problems did start on curve six. That's when I lost control. That's when I started hitting the walls. I've got to get back on the sled. I've got to get back on the sled. I can do it, I can do it, I can do it. I'm a winner, I'm a winner, I'm a winner. I WILL go to the Olympics."

Sometimes, I have to give myself a pep talk for fifteen to twenty minutes, until, finally, the belief kicks in, the courage kicks in, and I'm finally ready to listen to Coach. And I say to myself, "I will get on the sled. And when I do, I'm pointing my toes, my head's going back, I'm steering harder, harder, harder on curve six, and I look out. I'm going to have my best run ever."

And I did—I did.

I never would have made it Olympics without Coach. You know what he does for me? In fifteen seconds, he takes my eyes off the fear and puts my eyes back on the dream—the Olympics.

I knew that I needed to follow Coach, but I resisted it for three Olympics. I fought it. My need for control controlled me. It kept me from being my best.

Control & Letting Go

Why is it so hard to let go? Why is it so hard to follow the leader? The need for control comes from fear of failure, fear of the unknown, and sometimes even fear of success. Being in control feels safe. But being in control keeps you in your comfort zone. You can't improve if you're in your comfort zone.

Letting go is scary. But letting go gets you out of your comfort zone so you can improve. When I realized that being in control was hurting me, I was finally able to let go.

Fear of Speed

Six years after the Salt Lake City Olympics, I decided to start training for the Vancouver Olympics.

Only the top forty men would get to compete in Vancouver, not fifty like before. I was always ranked about forty-fifth, and I was by far the oldest competitor.

If I hoped to make it, I was going to have to do something I'd never done before. I was going to have to follow Coach's advice right away.

Coach said, "Ruben, I can't believe you're still scared. You've been doing the luge for over twenty-five years. What's going on in your head when you're sliding?"

I told him, "As I see those walls going faster and faster, I get tighter and tighter. I can't believe I can even steer at the bottom of the track, because by then, I'm stiff like a board."

Coach said, "You're focusing on the wrong thing. Luge isn't about speed. It's about who has the best time. You could get clocked at the fastest speed, but if you crash at the bottom, you lose the race. So, stop looking at the walls. They're just scaring you. Pretend you're wearing blinders, like a horse. Focus on a spot about thirty feet in front of you and think about what you need to do in every section of every curve to ensure you'll have the best time. If you change your focus, the fear will disappear."

It made sense. I needed to stop focusing on my circumstances, and I needed to start focusing on what I needed to do to succeed. I trusted coach. And for the first time ever, I followed his advice right away.

That night, I did about a hundred mind runs—visualization runs. I pretended that I had blinders on like a horse. I only focused on my driving. The next day, when I took my next run, the fear disappeared. It didn't reduce in intensity. It disappeared.

Changing the focus changed the experience.

Success is a Decision

Success is a decision. Sooner or later, you decide you're willing to do whatever it takes to get the job done. I decided to start following my coach's advice right away.

The faster I followed my coach's advice, the faster I improved. And I was able to do things no one had ever done before.

At the Vancouver Olympics, I became the first person to compete in four Winter Olympics in four different decades.

At sixty-one, I'm sliding better and more consistently than ever. I'm training to become the oldest Winter Olympian in history.

Best of all, I discovered that you don't lose yourself when you follow the leader. Rather, you can become better than you ever were before.

What About You?

What if, next time you're trying to achieve a big goal, you look for someone who'd already done what you wanted to do?

What if you just let go and followed their advice right away? And what if you shared this simple idea with your friends?

You'd create a better life, you'd start a ripple effect of success, and you'd make the world a better place.

**~ Ruben Gonzalez, 4X Olympian, Bestselling Author of *The Shortcut*,
Keynote Speaker**

RUBEN GONZALEZ

Ruben Gonzalez is a common man who achieved extraordinary things. He wasn't a gifted athlete. In school he was always the last kid picked to play sports. He didn't take up the sport of luge until he was 21. Four years and a few broken bones later, he was competing in the Calgary Winter Olympics. When he competed at the Vancouver Olympics at the age of 47, Ruben became the first person to ever compete in four Winter Olympics each in a different decade.

Since 2002 Ruben has spoken for over 100 of the Fortune 500 companies. His bestselling books have sold over 300,000 copies and have been translated to over 10 languages.

Ruben's incredible story takes people's excuses away and fills them with the belief and inspiration to face their challenges and fight for their goals and dreams.

www.TheLugeMan.com

HONORING DR. WAYNE DYER

DON GREEN

GO THE EXTRA MILE: THE KEYS OF SUCCESSFUL MENTORS

I am filled with immense appreciation for all the experiences and opportunities that have enriched my life. People sometimes ask why I continue doing what I do. The answer lies within my passion for learning, which remains strong—something my journey took many hard hours of hard work, persistence, and tireless searching to attain.

Growing up during the Great Depression, my family wasn't wealthy, but we were rich with values. My parents, both with only seventh-grade educations, taught me the value of hard work and integrity. Early on, I learned to earn what I desired by either mowing lawns for others or collecting and selling pop bottles. Each experience taught me self-reliance and found ways to earn extra cash—an experience that taught me self-reliance and having purpose.

A defining moment in my life occurred when I realized that men working in coal mines, like my father, earned their living at great physical expense. Realizing this led me down a new path—one where my mind, rather than physical labor, could earn money; books became my gateway into that new life, which I devoured enthusiastically.

My career in banking started modestly, yet with all of the tenacity that had defined me from childhood. When people told me they thought it unlikely I'd become president of a bank someday, my faith never wavered despite their doubt. For me, it wasn't simply about titles; rather, it was all about making an impactful contribution. Though my hourly wage started out modestly at $1.15 an hour compared with current standards, I found every opportunity for growth exciting, no matter if that meant long hours at work or taking on additional responsibilities without immediate benefits!

One of the greatest lessons I ever received early on came from one of my mentors who advised, "Do a bit extra each day, and one day you will achieve success most people only dream about." His words of advice stuck with me throughout my career—whether in banking, real estate, or any of the various businesses where I was involved; whenever needed, I made sure to go the extra mile.

My years in venture capital have taught me valuable lessons on finding purpose in everything you do and giving everything your all. Success doesn't just involve making money; it comes from seeing something you are truly passionate about that you give everything into. Once value creation begins to happen, then profits follow naturally.

One principle I have held dear throughout my life has been giving back. From providing free services to local schoolchildren to donating land to universities, helping others has always been one of my guiding lights. Giving isn't simply charity—rather, understanding reciprocity allows good deeds to reap dividends is something else altogether!

As I transitioned from banking to leading the Napoleon Hill Foundation, I brought with me my commitment to excellence. Promoting Napoleon Hill's teachings has been one of the most satisfying parts of my career. His principles for success, such as having both a burning desire and a specific purpose, have resonated deeply since I first read *Think and Grow Rich*. These principles don't just exist theoretically but provide real-world tools anyone can use to accomplish their goals.

At every turn of my career journey, I have come to appreciate that surrounding yourself with like-minded individuals is critical. True success cannot be attained alone—teamwork and collaboration are essential in attaining any form of achievement. Over time, working alongside some extraordinary individuals, we have accomplished things I would have never been capable of alone.

I am still learning and developing each day. Walking five miles daily helps improve both physical health and overall life discipline—it is a constant reminder that no matter your age or achievements, there's always room for growth!

As part of my work with the Napoleon Hill Foundation, my focus remains on helping others unlock their full potential. Through books, courses, or personal mentorship sessions, I aim to impart all that I've learned so others may also achieve success—this mission remains dearly personal for me, one I will pursue as long as possible.

Success doesn't depend on luck. It comes through hard work, perseverance, and the willingness to go the extra mile, all qualities that, if developed, can unlock endless potential in life.

Mentorship has been one of the key principles in my life that has taught and guided my success. From my early days of managing banks to leading the Napoleon Hill Foundation today, proper mentorship involves creating an environment where others can thrive on their journey toward fulfillment and find their own paths to achievement.

Mentorship Through Common Goals

As a bank manager, I used the principles of mentorship by encouraging my team and me to work toward shared goals. Our office succeeded not due to me alone; everyone felt connected as part of something greater. When our office earned points through company incentive programs, I ensured everyone received equal shares so as to foster an environment in which everyone felt their contributions mattered—this wasn't about being fair just for fairness' sake. Instead, it fostered an environment where every contributor felt appreciated; when people are part of a team, they tend to go that extra mile more often!

Napoleon Hill recognized this principle when discussing Mastermind groups; I have witnessed it many times myself. According to Hill, success can never be attained alone, and masterminding is more than simply gathering minds; instead, it involves working toward one collective vision in harmony toward its realization. The success of a mastermind depends on each member being committed to its vision as much as anything else a business or personal goal might present them with.

Leading by Example

I've long believed in leading by example as a mentor. When I began working at an underperforming bank, I rolled up my sleeves alongside them and got involved myself rather than simply telling employees what needed to be done. Over the years, I have learned the best way to mentor someone is by showing through your actions what it takes for someone else to succeed; telling someone persistence or taking ownership of their success are simply ineffective methods—they need to see this manifested in your life firsthand!

Mentorship also means making hard decisions with integrity and standing by them. I have made difficult choices throughout my career—from selling banks to publishing books—yet always approached these decisions with integrity. Success doesn't come through taking an easier route but instead through making hard but right choices that lead to lasting achievement.

Communication is Crucial

Communication is at the core of effective mentorship. From providing words of encouragement or advice to listening as someone shares their journey, communication builds trust between mentors and mentees. I make a point to communicate openly and honestly with everyone I work with. When managing delinquent accounts early in my career, I discovered that working closely with people, understanding their situations, and helping them find solutions were more likely to yield positive results while creating trust between us—essential components in any mentor-mentee relationship!

Supporting Personal Growth

An effective mentor fosters personal development. This involves challenging others to step outside their comfort zones, take risks, and pursue their personal goals with determination—helping them see and actively explore the potential within themselves. Napoleon Hill was known to promote his work on having a clear purpose and exerting consistent effort as principles that aid such progress. My role as a mentor involves leading others toward these principles so they may apply them in their lives as I guide people toward these ideals myself.

Mentorship involves much more than simply imparting knowledge or providing advice; it's about creating an environment where others can discover their talents, take responsibility for their successes, and realize their goals. Working toward shared objectives together while leading by example is also part of mentoring; communication, trust building, and encouraging personal development all play vital parts. Ultimately, it should enable others to become the best versions of themselves!

These principles and many more have guided my life throughout and continue to serve me today as I work at the Napoleon Hill Foundation. My hope is that by applying these mentorship principles yourself, you, too, may help others realize their full potential.

DON GREEN

Don Green is an American business entrepreneur, having built a successful savings bank, a real estate enterprise, and a host of other small and successful businesses in southwestern Virginia prior to his latest career with the Napoleon Hill Foundation.

As CEO of the Napoleon Hill Foundation, Don Green has energized the works of the famed author with a host of new books by noted authors, demonstrating how the principles of the late Mr. Hill work to advance the individual in network with others around the globe. He has demonstrated unique determination to expand knowledge of Mr. Hill's motivational work the world over.

Moreover, Don is a new global social entrepreneur. He has become one of the leading evangelists of entrepreneurial self-help through properly utilizing Mr. Hill's *Keys to Success* and *Think and Grow Rich*. He accepts nontraditional ideas, change, and foresight, which are tempered and bounded only by positive action. He is a realist with a visionary outlook.

Don is a goal-setter. He calibrates his goals and objectives carefully but routinely works with sound methodology with a dedicated fever to achieve success. He appreciates those around him and their goals, too. Don seeks to share in the vision of others and help them attain their aspirations in entrepreneurial endeavors if they have the potential for positive impact.

Don Green, a resident of Wise, Virginia, the birthplace of Napoleon Hill, brings nearly 45 years of banking, finance, and entrepreneurship experience to his role as Executive Director of the Napoleon Hill Foundation. His first youthful business venture was charging admission to see his pet bear—yes, the living, growling kind! Since 2000, Green has traveled worldwide and used his finance skills to grow the Foundation's funds to continue the Foundation's educational outreach to prisons.

Green has modeled leadership skills as a CEO and taught them through the PMA Science of Success course at the University of Virginia's College at Wise. Don specializes in discussing his personal experiences in leadership and providing audiences with proven methods of applying Dr. Hill's success philosophy to business. Dr. Peter Yun recently featured him in a presentation on the Importance of Entrepreneurship in a National Economy at a United Nations Forum.

Don M. Green is executive director of the Napoleon Hill Foundation and president of the foundation board at the University of Virginia-Wise. He became CEO of Black Diamond Savings Bank at 41 and studied under personal development master W. Clement Stone. He travels extensively, lecturing worldwide for the Foundation. Most recently, Mr. Green was featured in a United Nations forum on the importance of entrepreneurship within the national economy.

www.NapHill.org

HONORING DR. WAYNE DYER

"CHANGE THE WAY YOU LOOK AT THINGS AND THE THINGS YOU LOOK AT CHANGE."

~ DR. WAYNE DYER

HONORING DR. WAYNE DYER

AMY KEIDERLING

EMBRACING THE PRESENT MOMENT—LIFE IS NOW

*"Change the way you look at things and
the things you look at change."*
~ **Dr. Wayne Dyer**

As I reflect on my journey and the experiences that have shaped me, I realize that the mentors who have come into my life have been more than just guides—they have been lifelines, anchors, and sources of inspiration in moments of triumph and despair. The power of mentorship is profound; it's not just about receiving advice or direction but about the transformation that occurs when someone truly sees you for who you are and believes in your potential, even when you cannot see it yourself.

My journey with cancer, starting with that first phone call on March 17th, 2020, has been filled with lessons, each one more powerful than the last. However, the most significant lesson I've learned is the importance of living fully in the present moment, and this lesson was solidified through the wisdom of my mentors.

One mentor in particular, Elaine, who urged me to take action with her powerful words, "Life is now," taught me that every moment is a choice —a choice to live, to love, and to embrace the life that is unfolding before us, regardless of the circumstances. She didn't just give me advice; she held up a mirror that reflected my inner strength and resilience. Through her, I learned that life does not wait for us to be ready; it happens in real time, and it's up to us to decide how we respond.

But Elaine wasn't the first mentor to guide me, and she certainly wasn't the last. As I navigated the turbulent waters of cancer, COVID-19, and the challenges that life threw my way, other mentors stepped into my life, each bringing their unique perspective and wisdom. They reminded me that I am not alone, that my struggles are not in vain, and that the power to create the life I desire lies within me.

Dr. Wayne Dyer, a mentor through his words and teachings, once said, "Change the way you look at things, and the things you look at change." This quote resonated with me deeply during my second round of cancer. It wasn't just about battling the disease—it was about transforming my mindset, changing how I viewed my situation, and recognizing that every challenge is an opportunity to grow, learn, and become more than I ever thought possible.

In its truest form, mentorship is about seeing beyond the surface, beyond the immediate obstacles, and into the possibilities that lie within us. My mentors saw potential in me that I couldn't see at the time. They believed in my ability to survive and thrive, pushing me to look at my life from a different perspective. They taught me that my life wasn't just happening to me—it was happening for me.

Through their guidance, I learned to embrace each moment with gratitude, to approach each day with a sense of wonder and curiosity, and to trust in the journey, no matter how uncertain it seemed. I realized that the present moment is all we truly have, and it is in this moment that we have the power to make choices that will shape our future.

As I continue to navigate my road of life, with its twists, turns, and unexpected detours, I carry the lessons my mentors have taught me. I've learned that the most important thing we can do is live fully, embrace the present, and trust that everything we experience is leading us to where we need to be.

My journey isn't over—there will be more phone calls, more challenges, and more moments when I'll need to dig deep and find the strength to keep going. But I know that, with the support of my mentors, the love of my family, and the belief in myself that I have cultivated, I will continue to rise, overcome, and live my life with purpose and passion.

In the end, life is now. It's not something that happens later, when things are perfect or when we feel ready. It's happening right here, right now, amid the chaos, the uncertainty, and the beauty of it all. And it's up to us to seize it, to live it fully, and to become the people we were meant to be.

So, as I move forward, I do so with the knowledge that I am not alone. I am supported by the wisdom of those who have come before me, the love of those who stand beside me, and the strength within me. Life is now, and I choose to live it with all I am.

LIFE IS NOW! LIFE IS NOW! LIFE IS NOW!

AMY KEIDERLING

About Amy Keiderling: Amy Keiderling is a Rebel Soul Guide. She helps to navigate you to find your soul's purpose. Think of her as a co-pilot on the road of life. When the road gets bumpy, curvy, or just seems full of obstacles and detours, we will pull out our Rebel Roadmap and navigate it together.

Amy Keiderling is the owner of Rebel Roadmap, MOdville, as well as an adventure guide with MO Adventures. Amy has always been an avid collector of anything vintage; the instant connection a piece gives you to a memory or story is why she loves her fab finds & and creating memories. Amy's passion grew stronger when she met Keith, as his passion for custom vintage cars, motorcycles, and random collectibles grew their collection. When Amy and Keith are not taking adventure lovers on chartered vacations/ retreats, or riding around on their motorcycles, you will find them lounging in the middle of MOwhere on their 30-acre Mid-Century Modern Retreat Property. LIFE IS NOW! Amy's battle cry - as she's experienced life from everything from divorce, body image struggles, self-worth, bankruptcy, food stamps, single parenthood, starting 4 businesses, being a Rock Star Mom & Mimi to her Bigs & Littles, and a cancer warrior fighting Non-Hodgkin's Lymphoma! Amy's road may be "bumpy", but she's grateful for her "off road" adventure called LIFE. Amy encourages everyone to navigate their road of life and follow their inner GPS full of MO Adventures, MO Fun & MO Memories with the ones you love.

Author's Website: *www.ItsAMoAdventure.com* & *www.RebelRoadmap.com @RebelRoadmap*

Book Series Website: *www.TheBookOfMentors.com*

DR. ANGELA HARDEN-MACK, MD

MANIFEST YOUR GREATNESS: A JOURNEY TO FULFILLMENT & JOY

Wayne Dyer's book, *Manifest Your Destiny,* is a timeless guide that empowers us to align our thoughts, beliefs, and actions with a higher purpose. Through nine spiritual principles, Dyer offers a roadmap to a life filled with meaning, success, and deep fulfillment. As I reflect on these principles, I am inspired to share a concept I call "Great x3," which aligns beautifully with Dyer's teachings and provides a powerful framework for living a life of purpose, joy, influence, and impact.

Great x3 stands for, "You were created for greatness, to do great works, and to live a great life." This concept embodies the essence of our journey toward manifesting our destiny, echoing Dyer's profound message that each of us has the power within to create a life that I describe as the great life that glorifies our Creator, blesses those we serve, and satisfies us with good things. Great x3 focuses on three core aspects of our existence: Being, Doing, and Having—all of which are essential components of a fulfilled life.

The Call to Greatness: Understanding Your True Potential

In *Manifest Your Destiny*, Wayne Dyer emphasizes that the journey to manifesting our destiny begins with a deep understanding of our true potential. The first principle, "Believe in Yourself and Trust the Universe," is a powerful reminder that we are all inherently capable of achieving greatness. This belief is the foundation of Great x3: **You were created for greatness.** Each of us is a unique expression of divine creativity, with talents, abilities, and gifts that are meant to be shared with the world.

Believing in your greatness means recognizing that you are not a product of random chance but a deliberate creation with a specific purpose. This understanding shifts your perspective from one of limitation to one of limitless possibility. When you believe in your greatness, you align with the universal force that Dyer speaks of, opening yourself up to the flow of life that supports your highest aspirations.

The Power of Purposeful Action: Doing Great Works

The second aspect of Great x3 is to **do great works**. This aligns with Dyer's principles of "Align Your Desires with the Higher Self" and "Affirmations and the Power of Intention." Dyer teaches that our actions must be aligned with our spiritual purpose and that by setting clear, positive intentions, we direct our energy toward creating the life we desire.

Doing great works is about more than just achieving success in the conventional sense; it's about living a life of purpose and meaning. When your actions are guided by your higher self, you are not merely working for personal gain but contributing to the greater good. Every task, no matter how small, becomes an opportunity to express your divine purpose. This is the essence of living a life that blesses others, as your actions are in service to those you are called to help.

In the journey of manifesting your greatness, your actions are the bridge between your inner desires and your external reality. Dyer's principle of "Visualization and Imagination" emphasizes the importance of seeing your desired outcome in your mind's eye and taking inspired action to bring it into being. This is where mindfulness, or the power of the present moment, plays a crucial role. By staying grounded in the now, you ensure that your actions are aligned with your intentions and that you are fully present in the process of creating your destiny.

The Fulfillment of Having: Living a Great Life

The third and final aspect of Great x3 is **to live a great life**. This speaks to the ultimate goal of our journey: to experience a life of fulfillment, joy, and satisfaction. Dyer's principles of "Detachment from Outcomes" and "Living in the Present Moment" are particularly relevant here, as they teach us that true fulfillment comes not from chasing after external achievements but from cultivating a sense of inner peace and contentment.

Living a great life means embracing the present moment with gratitude and recognizing that every experience—whether joyful or challenging—is an opportunity for growth and self-discovery. Dyer's principle of "Gratitude as a Manifestation Tool" reminds us that when we appreciate the blessings in our lives, we attract more of the same. Gratitude shifts our focus from what we lack to what we have, creating a positive feedback loop that brings more abundance into our lives.

As a holistic wellness coach, I often see how the pursuit of achievement and success can be misunderstood as a relentless drive for perfection. However, Dyer's teachings and the concept of Great x3 emphasize that true fulfillment, greatness, is not about being perfect but about being authentic, aligned, and purposeful. Perfection is a falsehood; what matters is progress and the pursuit of what truly matters.

The Journey to Your Greatness & Great Life

Reflecting on Dyer's book, I am inspired to summarize it as a call to embark on a journey of your ever evolving greatness. This journey is deeply personal, grounded in the understanding that you discover and embrace all of you, and to live your great life is not something to be found outside of yourself but something to be created from within. Dyer's nine principles provide the tools to navigate this journey, helping you align your thoughts, inner self, and inner self-talk with your highest aspirations.

The journey of greatness is one of self-discovery, growth, and transformation. It is about embracing who you are, taking inspired action to bring your dreams to life, and living with the awareness that every moment is an opportunity to manifest your destiny. Mindfulness, or the power of the present moment, is the anchor that keeps you grounded in this journey, allowing you to move forward with confidence, clarity, and purpose.

Embracing Your Greatness

Everyone has a destiny to be great. Your greatness is not just for your benefit but also for the glory of your Creator, the blessing of those you are meant to serve, and the fulfillment of your own soul. When you embrace your greatness, you live a life of purpose, joy, influence, and impact.

Wayne Dyer's, *Manifest Your Destiny,* is a powerful reminder that the process of manifesting your destiny is within your control, guided by your thoughts, beliefs, and actions. By embracing the principles he outlines and applying the Great x3 framework, you can create a life that not only fulfills your deepest desires but also contributes to the greater good. This is the essence of living a great life—a life of fulfillment, joy, and satisfaction that resonates with your true purpose.

As you embark on your journey to BE great, remember that you were created for greatness, to do great works, and to live a great life. Embrace your greatness with confidence and watch as your destiny unfolds before you, bringing you closer to the life you were always meant to live.

DR. ANGELA HARDEN-MACK, MD

About Dr. Angela Harden-Mack, MD: Dr. Angela Harden-Mack, MD, is a woman on a mission serving ambitious success-oriented career women. Dr. Angela uses her keynote to motivate women to take action to release the stressful and pressured Superwoman lifestyle to be healthier and happier enjoying personal and professional success. Dr. Angela, wellness expert, women's empowerment coach, international speaker, and entrepreneur, has been featured in print and broadcast media.

Learn more about Dr. Angela and her company, Live Great Lives, at *www.drangela360.com.*

Author's Website: *www.LiveGreatLives.com*

Book Series Website: www.TheBookOfMentors.com

AZADEH BENNETT
THE POWER OF CHOICE

"Be miserable. Or motivate yourself. Whatever has to be done, it's always your choice."
~ **Dr. Wayne Dyer**

These days, it's hard not to notice how much people love to complain. The economy, politics, the place they live, their jobs, even their families and spouses—nothing seems safe from a good grumble. I should know; I used to be one of them. But here's the twist—I was also grateful. Grateful for the roof over my head, the food on my table, and the people in my life. It's funny how you can be both grateful and miserable at the same time, isn't it?

There's a beautiful poem by Sa'adi, a famous poet from Iran, written way back in the 10th century, that has stuck with me. He wrote that, with every breath we take, there are two praises to God: one for the inhale, and one for the exhale. It's a poetic way of saying that even the simple act of breathing is something to be grateful for. Think about that for a second—every breath, every single one, is an opportunity to give thanks. Imagine living in such a state of gratitude that you're thanking the universe for every inhale and exhale. That's where I've found myself these days.

Now, don't get me wrong—I'm far from living my dream life. But that doesn't stop me from being grateful for where I am right now. I'm creating my life, moment by moment, with every choice I make. It wasn't always this way. Not long ago, I was stuck in a job that made me feel miserable. I was constantly surrounded by negativity, and it seeped into my soul, making me feel like there was no escape. But then, something changed.

I realized that I had the power to choose. I could either stay miserable, complaining about my circumstances, or I could motivate myself to change. I chose the latter. And let me tell you, it wasn't easy. But it was worth it.

Now, as I look back, I see that every experience, every hardship, was preparing me for something greater. When God closed that chapter of my life, He opened doors to opportunities I never could have imagined. And I chose to walk through them. Today, I'm on a path that aligns with who I was meant to be—someone who stands for freedom, not just for myself, but for nations and women around the world.

As you continue reading, you'll see what I mean. I'll share with you the journey I'm on, the impact I'm making, and the purpose I've discovered. It's a story of transformation, of choosing to create the life I want, and of finding gratitude even in the smallest of moments. So, stick with me, because we're just getting started. There's so much more to share, and I promise it will be worth it.

The Power of Reaction

"How people treat you is their karma; how you react is yours."
~ Dr. Wayne Dyer

I'm so glad I've come to understand the wisdom in this quote from Wayne Dyer. It's like a lightbulb moment that suddenly makes everything click. Dyer often used a simple yet profound analogy to explain this concept. He'd ask, "What do you get if you squeeze an orange?" The obvious answer: orange juice. But then he'd ask, "Why do you get orange juice and not apple juice when you squeeze an orange?" The answer, of course, is because orange juice is what's inside the orange —not apple juice, not grape juice, just orange juice.

This metaphor applies to our lives as well. When we're under pressure, stressed, angry, or even just tired and hungry, what's inside us comes out.

If we're filled with love, understanding, and patience, that's what will spill over. But if we're full of resentment, anger, or bitterness, well, that's what will come pouring out instead.

Understanding this principle was a big part of my self-discovery journey. I've reached a point where I can see what's inside me, especially when life squeezes me. And if my reaction isn't what I'd hoped, I can look back and find the source of that reaction. It's like a built-in self-reflection tool that helps me stay true to who I want to be.

I remember when I was at my last job. I had this feeling that my time there was winding down. I prayed for guidance and asked God to show me what to do, but no clear direction came. Then, out of the blue, they told me I was being laid off. Now, for most people, that would be terrible news, but for me? It was like a weight had been lifted off my shoulders. I felt pure joy and energy, like an eagle soaring at 10,000 feet. I couldn't sleep because I was so excited about the opportunities ahead.

That layoff was a blessing in disguise. My previous job just didn't have the space for my ideas and creativity. Their karma was letting me go; mine was to embrace the freedom and creativity that came with it. I stepped into this unknown world of possibilities, curious and determined not to let this change be anything but positive.

Since then, I've explored so many new fields—coaching, consulting, training, and now, my creative work with AI and YouTube. It's been an incredible journey, and I'm still discovering all the amazing things I can do with AI. I've found a way to share my passion for Persian mythology and storytelling through YouTube, blending creativity with technology in ways I never imagined.

Every day, I wake up excited to paint my life's blank canvas with joy, creativity, and freedom. And now, my vision is to help others find their identity and purpose in life, too. That's my mission, and I know it's one I will accomplish. We all have the power to choose our reactions and create the life we desire. I'm living proof of that.

The Power of Belief

"If you believe it will work out, you'll see opportunities. If you believe it won't, you will see obstacles."
~ Dr. Wayne Dyer

We all know someone who, no matter what idea you share, immediately points out all the reasons it won't work. They see obstacles where you see opportunities, and their negativity can be exhausting. I have a few of those people close to me. While their constant focus on the risks can drain my energy, I remind myself that they come from a place of love and concern. They're not trying to hold me back—they're just wired to see the world differently. So, I listen to their concerns, but I don't let them weigh me down. Instead, I consider their warnings as potential risks, but nothing more than that.

I'm blessed to have been raised by a father who was the opposite—he was all about possibilities, opportunities, and big visions. He encouraged me to dream big and see the world as a place full of potential. One of his greatest gifts to me was planting the seed of living in the U.S. when I was just a kid in Iran. He believed it would work out, and because of that belief, I saw all the opportunities in making that move. My life in the U.S. has been a roller coaster, but I'm grateful for every moment that has brought me to where I am today.

Now, I hold a vision of a world filled with peace, joy, creativity, and freedom. I see myself as a source of inspiration and a beacon of freedom for the people of Iran. One of my deepest passions is to introduce the epic stories of *Shahnameh* by the great Iranian poet Ferdowsi to the world. These mythical stories are a reminder of our ancestors' strength, wisdom, and the blessings that have shaped Iran into what it is today. They also serve as a powerful symbol for the people of Iran to stand against the brutal regime and reclaim their freedom.

I believe this vision will work out, and I'm taking steps every day to make it a reality. With the help of AI, I'm creating these stories and plan to share them on YouTube, gradually bringing *Shahnameh* to life in a way that resonates with a global audience. At the same time, I'm working on a feature film screenplay based on the first major story in *Shahnameh*, with the goal of turning it into a globally recognized movie or animation. Wayne Dyer once said, "When you change the way you look at things, the things you look at change." I've changed the way I look at life, and in doing so, I've become a permission slip for others, especially those in Iran, to see life differently. I stand firm in this vision, knowing that the Lord has my back. He's the one who planted this dream in my heart, and I'm ready to take on this next stage of my life with all the courage and determination I have.

In this journey of self-discovery and growth, I've shared how the teachings of Wayne Dyer have profoundly influenced my life. From understanding the power of choice, to mastering my reactions, to believing in the possibilities that lie ahead, Dyer's wisdom has been a guiding light.

Through these chapters, I've reflected on the importance of gratitude, the impact of mindset, and the power of belief in shaping our reality. My vision of freedom for Iran and my creative endeavors with AI and storytelling are all rooted in these principles. I hope my story inspires others to believe in themselves, see the opportunities before them, and create a life filled with purpose, joy, and freedom.

AZADEH BENNETT

About Azadeh Bennett: Azadeh Bennett is a creative leader and transformational coach, specializing in harnessing generative AI and creativity to empower individuals and organizations. With a rich background in emotional intelligence, strategic communication, and design thinking, Azadeh helps others unlock their potential and drive meaningful change.

Azadeh's dedication is strengthened by her loving marriage to Jason Bennett, whose unwavering support fuels her passion for transformation and freedom. Together, they exemplify the power of love and partnership in pursuing life's purpose. Armed with master's degrees in MBA, Strategic Communication, and Global Studies, Azadeh blends her knowledge and expertise to guide clients in leveraging their strengths, fostering creativity, and developing innovative solutions to challenges. Her passion for personal and professional growth is evident in every aspect of her work.

Azadeh's vision extends beyond her professional endeavors. She is dedicated to championing freedom and creativity, particularly for women in Iran. Through her work on bringing the mythical epic stories of *Shahnameh* to life using AI and YouTube, she aims to inspire a global audience and remind the people of Iran of their rich heritage and the power of freedom.

A visionary strategist, Azadeh draws inspiration from the world around her. She expresses her creativity through playing the harp, painting, and exploring the possibilities of AI. Her multidisciplinary approach reflects her belief in the transformative power of creativity and innovation.

Author's Website: *www.AzadehBennett.com*

Book Series Website: *www.TheBookOfMentors.com*

DR. BETTY SPEAKS

CONFIDENCE: THE KEY TO UNLEASHING YOUR FULL POTENTIAL

Imagine a world where every step you take is filled with certainty, every word you speak resonates with power, and every challenge you face is met with an unwavering belief in your abilities.

This is the world of confidence—a realm where dreams become realities and limitations transform into boundless possibilities. Are you ready to step into this world?

Confidence has been the cornerstone of my journey through life. From personal achievements to professional milestones, it has played an essential role in every endeavor.

Confidence is not merely about self-assurance; it is about having faith in your abilities, trusting your instincts, and daring to take bold steps even when the path ahead is uncertain.

This chapter delves into the essence of confidence, how it has shaped my life, and how it can become your most powerful tool.

The Power of Confidence in Life's Endeavors

At the age of twenty-two, I faced one of the most daunting challenges of my life: starting my own business. The idea of leaving a stable job to pursue my passion was terrifying. I had no guarantee of success, and the fear of failure loomed large. But I remembered the words of Wayne Dyer, "You are not stuck where you are unless you decide to be." With these words echoing in my mind, I took the fearless leap into entrepreneurship.

A Strategic Takeaway: Embrace uncertainty with confidence. Trust in your abilities and take calculated risks. Steps to success:

1. **Identify Your Passion:** Know what drives you and align your goals with your passions.

2. **Plan & Prepare:** Develop a solid business plan and prepare for potential challenges.

3. **Take the Leap:** Once prepared, take the bold step forward with confidence.

"Go confidently in the direction of your dreams. Live the life you have imagined."
~ Henry David Thoreau

"For I know the plans I have for you, declares the Lord, plans to prosper you and not to harm you, plans to give you hope and a future."
~ Jeremiah 29:11

Taking the Bold Step Toward Becoming a Public Speaker

Public speaking was never my forte. The thought of standing in front of an audience and delivering a speech filled me with dread. However, I knew that to advance in my career, I had to conquer this fear. With determination and confidence, I enrolled in a public speaking course. Each speech I delivered, no matter how small the audience, built my confidence. I soon found myself speaking at conferences and inspiring others with my words.

A Strategic Takeaway: Confidence is built through practice and persistence. Steps to success:

1. **Start Small:** Begin with small audiences to build your confidence.

2. **Seek Feedback:** Learn from constructive criticism and continually improve.

3. **Practice Regularly:** Consistent practice helps to refine your skills and boost confidence.

"If you believe it will work out, you'll see opportunities. If you believe it won't, you will see obstacles."
~ Dr. Wayne Dyer

"I can do all things through Christ who strengthens me."
~ Philippians 4:13

A Personal Triumph

When I was thirteen, I faced significant personal challenges that tested my confidence. Bullying and self-doubt made me question my worth. However, with the support of a mentor and my unwavering faith, I learned to see myself through the eyes of possibility rather than limitation. This early lesson in confidence laid the foundation for my future successes.

Know that confidence is often forged in the fires of adversity.

Here are a few steps to keep your confidence:

1. **Seek Support:** Surround yourself with mentors and supportive individuals who believe in you.

2. **Develop Self-Belief:** Focus on your strengths and accomplishments to build self-esteem.

3. **Stay Resilient:** Use setbacks as steppingstones to build greater confidence. Wayne Dyer said, "When you judge another, you do not define them; you define yourself." A good Scripture to follow: "But they who wait for the Lord shall renew their strength; they shall mount up with wings like eagles; they shall run and not be weary; they shall walk and not faint." – Isaiah 40:31

In summary, confidence is the catalyst that transforms dreams into reality. It empowers you to take risks, face challenges, and pursue your goals with unwavering belief. Reflecting on the thirteen-year-old Betty Speaks, I see a young girl who, despite her fears and doubts, learned to trust in her abilities and embrace her potential.

Today, as a mentor and motivational speaker, I strive to instill this same confidence in others.

I invite you to embark on your journey toward confidence. Therefore, reach out to me for mentorship, and let's work together to unlock your full potential. Remember, confidence is not a destination; it is a journey.

Each step you take, no matter how small, brings you closer to the empowered, confident individual you are meant to be.

Resources to Support this Chapter:

- **Books:** *The Power of Now* by Eckhart Tolle, *The Confidence Code* by Katty Kay and Claire Shipman

- **Courses:** Public speaking courses, confidence-building workshops

- **Podcasts:** Motivational leadership podcasts featuring interviews with successful leaders

- **Mentorship Programs:** Personalized mentorship sessions to guide you on your journey to confidence. Together, we can build a future where confidence is not just a trait but a way of life. Reach out to me today, and let's start this transformative journey. You can connect with me by visiting: *www.BettySpeaks.com*

DR. BETTY SPEAKS

About Dr. Betty Speaks: Dr. Speaks is a United States Army retiree, the CEO of A Life Change NOW, and Podcast Host of Overcoming Battles by Being Strong and Courageous. The Artist/ Songwriter of the Single *It's A Resurrection*. She is your Lifetime IMPRINT EMPRESS! She is very passionate about MOTIVATING individuals to resurrect and establish themselves spiritually, personally, or professionally. She's that chosen warrior who inspires others to create A Life Change Now by leaving an INTENTIONAL IMPACTFUL IMPRINT for INFINITY.

Betty is extremely passionate about helping individuals establish themselves and their generational wealth through multiple streams of income and secure their retirement endeavors. She also mentors youthful ladies and other individuals or teams during transformational workshops, one-on-one mentorship, and other total well-being events. Betty Speaks "IT" when she speaks.

Author's Website: *www.BettySpeaks.com*

Book Series Website: *www.TheBookOfMentors.com*

HONORING DR. WAYNE DYER

"PRACTICE BEING THE KIND OF PERSON YOU WISH TO ATTRACT."

~ DR. WAYNE DYER

BOPI VILLARINO

THE TRANSFORMATIVE POWER OF MENTORSHIP

Mentorship is a powerful, transformative experience that extends far beyond the mere exchange of knowledge and skills. It's about creating a lasting impact on another person's life, guiding them through challenges, celebrating their successes, and empowering them to reach their highest potential. My journey in the world of mentorship has been one of the most fulfilling aspects of my professional and personal life, deeply rooted in the wisdom imparted by those who have mentored me and the lessons I've learned along the way.

Reflecting on the mentors who have shaped my journey, one stands out with particular resonance—Dr. Wayne Dyer. His teachings have significantly influenced my understanding of mentorship and its profound role in our lives. Dr. Dyer once said, "If you change the way you look at things, the things you look at change." This quote encapsulates a truth I have found time and again in mentorship: the most profound transformations often begin with a simple shift in perspective.

Mentorship Through the Lens of Perspective

When we look at mentorship through this lens, we see it as more than just guiding someone along a path. It's about helping them see the world in a new light, offering perspectives that can alter the course of their lives. As a mentor, my role has been to illuminate possibilities, to encourage my mentees to see beyond their current circumstances, and to inspire them to envision and pursue a future they might not have thought possible.

One of the most significant ways I've impacted my mentees is by helping them reframe their challenges. Often, the hurdles we face seem insurmountable, not because of their size but because of the way we perceive them. By helping my mentees shift their perspective—from viewing challenges as obstacles to seeing them as opportunities for growth—I've witnessed them overcome seemingly impossible odds. This shift in mindset is the essence of mentorship, as it empowers individuals to take control of their narratives and chart their own paths forward.

Building Bridges to Success

In my own life, I've been fortunate to have mentors who helped me build bridges to success by offering advice and providing the tools and perspectives needed to navigate the complexities of life and business. From my early days in real estate to my experiences as a business coach, these mentors have been instrumental in shaping the person I've become. They've taught me that success is not a destination but a journey that requires constant growth, learning, and adaptation.

As I reflect on the lessons imparted by mentors like Brian Tracy and Bob Proctor, I am reminded of the importance of integrating personal development with practical strategies. Both men emphasized the power of the mind and the necessity of aligning our thoughts with our actions. They showed me that mentorship is about imparting knowledge and fostering a mindset that encourages continual improvement and resilience.

This holistic approach has become the foundation of my mentorship philosophy. I believe that to mentor someone truly, we must help them develop the skills needed for success and the mindset that will sustain them through life's inevitable ups and downs. This means guiding them through practical challenges while nurturing their personal growth and emotional well-being.

The Impact Beyond Mentorship

One of the most rewarding aspects of mentorship is witnessing the ripple effect it creates. When we mentor someone, we don't just impact their life—we also influence the lives of those they touch. This ripple effect can be seen in how my mentees approach their careers, relationships, and contributions to their communities.

By sharing the lessons I've learned and the perspectives I've gained, I've watched my mentees go on to mentor others, creating a chain of positive influence that extends far beyond our initial interactions. This, to me, is the true power of mentorship: the ability to inspire others to become mentors themselves, perpetuating a cycle of growth, empowerment, and transformation.

Cultivating a Mentorship Mindset

In cultivating a mentorship mindset, I encourage my mentees to embrace continuous learning, remain open to new ideas, and always seek ways to improve themselves and their surroundings. This mindset is beneficial not only in their professional lives but also in their personal development. It's about seeing every experience as an opportunity to learn and grow, about recognizing that mentorship is a lifelong journey.

Mentorship, as I've come to understand it, is about more than just guiding someone toward their goals. It's about helping them become the best version of themselves, empowering them to achieve their dreams while staying true to their values and principles. It's about creating a legacy of wisdom, compassion, and integrity that will continue to inspire and uplift others long after we've moved on to new challenges and opportunities.

The Legacy of Mentorship

As I look back on my journey, I am grateful for the mentors who have guided me and the mentees who have trusted me to guide them. Mentorship has been a cornerstone of my personal and professional life, shaping who I am today and who I will continue to become. It's a journey that has taught me the value of perspective, the importance of growth, and the power of influence.

In the words of Dr. Wayne Dyer, "If you change the way you look at things, the things you look at change." This simple yet profound truth has guided my approach to mentorship and continues to inspire me as I help others navigate their paths. By embracing this mindset, I hope to leave a lasting impact on those I mentor, empowering them to change the way they see the world and, in doing so, to change their world for the better.

BOPI VILLARINO

About Bopi Villarino: Raised in the picturesque La Costa Carlsbad, California, Bopi, has always been driven by a passion for education and real estate. She holds a Bachelor of Arts Degree in Liberal Studies/Elementary Education from Point Loma Nazarene University. As a dedicated mother to her beloved son Ross Villarino and cherished daughter-in-law Chelsea, Bopi takes pride in her role as a family-oriented individual. Bopi's remarkable journey into the world of real estate commenced at the young age of 18 when she served as a real estate assistant to a top-producing agent. She then ventured into the financial sector, establishing a mortgage company and expanding into the realms of real estate and escrow services.

After 15 years, Bopi successfully sold their business to a prominent nationwide brand. Bopi continued to soar in her career, assuming pivotal roles such as Vice President of the Western Region for a division of Lending Tree and Managing Partner for a substantial team in the bustling city of Los Angeles. Her versatile skill set encompasses positions such as manager, director of sales, and team lead across various real estate companies, spanning Southern California, Vail, Colorado, and Park City, Utah. Bopi became a certified real estate coach, extending her expertise to business owners and agents throughout the nation. Bopi took the courageous step of resigning from her role as the Utah Principal State Broker, where she oversaw a thriving community of 600+ agents. She founded Distinctive Properties, a real estate company nestled in the scenic beauty of Heber City, Utah. She finds solace and fulfillment in being in nature, and in various activities, including waterskiing, skiing/snowboarding, hiking, SUPing, snowshoeing, and camping.

Author's Website: *www.DistinctivePropertiesUtah.com*

Book Series Website: *www.TheBookOfMentors.com*

HONORING DR. WAYNE DYER

DANIEL KILBURN

LIFE IS NOW: WAYNE DYER PHILOSOPHY

Unveiling the Essence of Self-Development

Affectionately regarded as the "father of motivation," Dr. Wayne Dyer has etched a permanent place in self-help and personal growth. This chapter explores how his life's work has inspired countless individuals to achieve greater fulfillment and happiness.

My first encounter with Dyer's work was through a recording of, *The Secrets of Manifesting Your Destiny* from the '90s. This wasn't just an audio preference over radio; it was a conduit for profound life insights during times of personal strife. Listening to the author's own voice conveyed nuances and emotions beyond the printed word, offering greater intimacy with the material.

The Encounter with Destiny's Secrets

Why did *The Secrets of Manifesting Your Destiny* resonate so strongly? I was in a period filled with personal challenges, void of purpose or direction. The proposition of actualizing one's destiny by intention and action struck a chord—it was empowering. The allure of shaping one's destiny wasn't unfamiliar, but its practice became a foundational truth. Just like you, I embraced the responsibility for the life we carve out for ourselves.

*"Within you is a divine capacity to manifest and attract
all that you need or desire."*
~ Dr. Wayne Dyer

Formative Years & Philosophical Beginnings: Origins of Resilience

Born against the gritty backdrop of Detroit, Michigan, Dyer's trials from an early age molded his future teachings of perseverance and resilience. My own education in personal development began in the military during the 1970s—a time when leadership was both taught and learned. The quest for deeper knowledge often becomes interwoven with military life, sparking a yearning for personal enlightenment.

The pursuit of purpose isn't universal; yet, doesn't its necessity lie at the heart of shaping a world worth inhabiting? Society may seem intent on quelling individualism, but the choice to seek enlightenment remains a profoundly personal one. What kind of enlightenment do you seek?

Influential Beginnings

The combination of Dyer's academic pursuit and military service laid down the bedrock for his viewpoints on determination and positive awareness. His voice—soothing and insightful—resonated with me, affirming a universal beingness consistent with all creation. He highlighted life's adversities as catalysts to enlightenment, suggesting that they teach us the value of transcending through positivity.

Dyer's Foundational Teachings: The Potent Force of Intention

Wayne Dyer's philosophy, with its emphasis on the power of intention and the inherent ability of individuals to manifest their own realities, continues to resonate in today's fast-paced, often turbulent world. In an age where external circumstances frequently feel out of our control, Dyer's teachings offer a compelling narrative about the power of the mind and the capacity of thought to shape one's destiny.

By advocating for an inside-out approach to life—and suggesting that real change begins with a shift in individual consciousness—his work encourages a reevaluation of how we perceive challenges, success, and personal fulfillment. This philosophy is not only relevant but necessary, as it empowers individuals to reclaim agency over their lives, fostering a sense of peace and purpose amidst the chaos of the external world.

At the core of Dyer's message was the conviction that the power of intention underpins our existence. He proposed that our lives are formed by our intentions, and by aligning them with the universal good, we can achieve remarkable life transformations.

We are often criticized for self-serving intentions, influenced by cultural beliefs that regard enrichment as detrimental to morality. Dyer daringly challenged this, implying that such beliefs keep many in a state of impoverishment.

"The way you look at life is essentially a barometer of your expectations, based on what you've been taught you're worthy of and capable of achieving."
~ Dr. Wayne Dyer

The Welcome of Change

Welcoming the unpredictable was Dyer's formula for personal evolution. He urged acceptance of uncertainty as an avenue to uncharted opportunities, presenting a conundrum to our intrinsic resistance to change. Our own egos, much like our peers', often resist our advancement. Dyer's philosophy encourages breaching comfort zones, propelling us toward a greater potential.

In capturing the essence of Dyer's teachings for our co-authored book, we're reminded that life indeed is NOW—an immediate canvas upon which our intentions, shaped by knowledge and experience, have the power to paint a future of fulfillment and joy. As co-authors, we channel Dyer's enduring legacy into a narrative of empowerment and purpose-driven existence.

Wayne Dyer's Comprehensive Contributions

Wayne Dyer's legacy endures through a collection of works that distill his profound philosophies into accessible insights. The must-have "Essential Wayne Dyer Collection" integrates his pivotal writings, offering readers a guide to personal transformation. Each page serves as a beacon, leading the way to a life redefined by mental and spiritual growth.

Translating Ancient Wisdom for Today's World

In "Change Your Thoughts—Change Your Life," Dyer bridges centuries, connecting the ancient wisdom of the Tao Te Ching to the modern quest for fulfillment. Advocating for a radical shift in mindset, he proposes that our path to joy lies in the way we see the world.

The Power to Manifest

Diving deeper into self-actualization, *Manifest Your Destiny* reveals the potential to harness universal energy. Dyer prompts us to align our spirit with the cosmos, thus unlocking our ability to realize ambitions and tap into untapped potential.

Implementing Dyer's Methods: Everyday Practices for Inner Change

Wayne Dyer's books aren't mere narratives; they're handbooks for those intent on nurturing their inner selves. Whether through meditation or conscious intention, Dyer encouraged us to look inward and assert that real change stems from within. His strategies aren't shrouded in mystery or complexity but call for a commitment to daily reflection and action.

Reflecting on these methods, it's clear they are both approachable and practical—intention and introspection are the cornerstones. By shifting our beliefs and nurturing our thoughts, we initiate a ripple effect of personal evolution.

Tackling Life's Obstacles

Dyer's philosophies offer solace and strength to those wrestling with challenges. The mantra "Life is Now!" grounds us in the present, steering us away from the temptation to revisit the past or lose ourselves in unfounded futures. This focus on the immediacy of life fuels our actions with purpose and vitality.

Ripples of Influence: Impacting Leaders & Laypeople Alike

Dyer's influence permeates the field of self-help, where prominent minds attribute their own clarity and success to his instruction. However, his reach extends beyond the personal development sphere; his wisdom prompts us to contemplate our effect on others. From thought leaders to everyday interactions, our influence is a reflection of the power of intention.

Transformations in the Professional Sphere

The business community, too, has felt Dyer's touch. His frameworks for intention have reshaped corporate strategies, fostering enhanced productivity and a healthier occupational atmosphere. No matter our role or industry, harnessing a driven, purposeful approach to challenges offers a compass for navigating professional complexities.

For those questioning the relevance of Dyer's principles in a non-professional context, consider professional strategies for success mirror those needed in daily life. The pursuit of excellence, be it in parenting, homemaking, or culinary arts, is grounded in practice and persistence. Every expert was once a beginner, and every masterful feat began with a single, tentative step. We cannot solve our problems with the same level of belief that created them.

"You leave old habits behind by starting out with the thought, 'I release the need for this in my life.'"
~ Dr. Wayne Dyer

A Balanced View: Addressing the Skeptics

Even amidst acclaim, Dyer's methodologies have encountered skepticism, particularly concerning the empirical evidence supporting his approaches. This scrutiny mirrors the broader debates over spiritual and self-help disciplines throughout history—where tangible proof isn't always available, yet millions can testify to the transformations they have experienced.

My personal voyage through manifestation and self-discovery echoes Dyer's sentiments. Although reality may not shift at the mere flick of a finger, the steadfast pursuit of self-actualization—crafted over years of trial and triumph—continues to shape our journeys.

Carrying Forward a Visionary's Dream

Wayne Dyer's teachings remain a testament to the undeniable power of self-improvement. His vision defines an industry and continues to light the way for aspirants of a fulfilled, enlightened existence.

Wayne Dyer carved a niche within the personal development landscape, presenting an approach that melded spiritual depth with actionable guidance. This chapter celebrates his teachings—not as distant doctrines but as living practices that continue to nurture souls in the ongoing adventure of personal growth. Let us heed Dyer's words and "never die with our music still in us," but, instead, embrace a life of purposeful intention.

In the pursuit of personal growth, I've discovered that a synergetic approach to self-improvement yields profound insights. Melding the wisdom of Wayne Dyer with other pillars of personal development has not only shifted my perspective but also influenced how others perceive me.

To cultivate a successful self-improvement practice, there are three pivotal strategies to consider:

First, construct a well-defined plan. This blueprint will serve as your guide, helping to direct your progress with intention and focus.

Second, engage with the process playfully. Infusing playfulness into your growth can transform the arduous task of self-improvement into a delightful adventure.

Lastly, remain steadfast in your quest. Persistence is the key that unlocks the potential within; it fortifies your commitment to continual growth, despite the inevitable obstacles.

Incorporating these strategies into your daily routine will enrich your life and empower you on your remarkable path of personal evolution.

"Let the world know why you're here, and do it with passion."
~ Dr. Wayne Dyer

DANIEL KILBURN

About Daniel Kilburn: Daniel Kilburn, America's "5-Star Leadership Coach," is a speaker, author, and coach on the topics of Communications, Leadership, Financial Literacy, and Disaster Planning. Daniel will open communications, build resiliency, and develop leadership by preparing you, your family, and your organization to have tough conversations.

Daniel's mission is "Empowering resilience and leadership through proactive communication and disaster preparedness." Put a plan in place and act on it. Dream, Develop, and Deliver.

Daniel is the Urban Disaster Planning Expert with over 30 years of experience training young men and women, foreign nationals, and Department of Defense Civilians to survive on the modern battlefield. His current focus is on Financial Literacy. He is the author of *Family Urban Disaster Planning* and *Commanding Your Future* and co-author of the #1 Bestsellers, *The Book of Influence, a*nd *The Book of Mentors.* He earned his MBA with a minor in Project Management while serving in the U.S. Army as a single father.

Daniel has been featured in *Authority Magazine, Lifestyles over 50*, and *WFLA News Channel 8*. In addition to working one-on-one, he teaches live in-person and online events. It is his duty, obligation, and responsibility to tell you the truth.

Author's Website: *www.DanielKilburn.com*

Book Series Website: *www.TheBookOfMentors.com*

DAWNESE OPENSHAW

THE TRANSFORMATIVE INFLUENCE & LEGACY OF WAYNE DYER

Mentorship is more than imparting knowledge; it's about igniting a spark within, fostering growth, and transforming lives. In the realm of self-improvement and personal growth, few have made as profound an impact as Wayne Dyer. Known as the "father of motivation," Wayne Dyer's teachings have inspired millions to transcend their limitations, embrace their true potential, and live with purpose. His mentorship journey is a testament to the power of guidance, authenticity, and the belief that we each hold the key to our own transformation.

Wayne Dyer's influence extended beyond conventional mentorship. He was a beacon of light, guiding individuals through the murky waters of self-doubt, fear, and complacency. His philosophy centered on the idea that our thoughts create our reality, and by shifting our mindset, we can change our lives. This simple yet profound principle became the cornerstone of his teachings, and his unwavering belief in human potential transformed countless lives.

Practical Wisdom for Everyday Life

Wayne Dyer's teachings were not just theoretical; they were practical and applicable to everyday life. He offered tools and techniques that individuals could use to navigate their challenges and create positive change. From affirmations and visualization exercises to mindfulness practices and meditation, Dyer's toolbox was rich with resources for personal growth.

One of his most practical teachings was the idea of "acting as if." Dyer encouraged people to act as if they already had what they desired, to embody the qualities and behaviors they aspired to cultivate. This practice of "acting as if" helps to shift our mindset and align our actions with our intentions, creating a powerful momentum for change.

This has created a powerful shift for me when I set goals, particularly BIG and lofty goals. On the journey of accomplishing my goals, I have doubts creep in, saying, "Who are you to do this?" or "What makes you special enough to be heard through all the other voices out there?"

It's human nature to have these thoughts and what makes all the difference is what you DO with the thoughts. Do you allow them to take over and create a spiral of self-doubt or stop them in their tracks and intentionally choose what to do next from a space of your vision? Seeing it as it is already DONE makes a world of difference.

The impact mentors like Wayne Dyer have made on me is seeing how I can shift from a space of doubt to one where I feel empowered in my choices and focused, driven even, on what matters most to me.

The Role of Spirituality in Personal Growth

Spirituality was a central theme in Wayne Dyer's mentorship. He believed that personal growth and spiritual development are intertwined and that true transformation comes from connecting with our higher self. This connection to the divine is what gives us the strength and guidance to overcome our challenges and live our purpose.

Dyer's spiritual teachings were inclusive and universal, drawing from various traditions and philosophies. He spoke about the importance of love, compassion, and forgiveness, and he encouraged individuals to cultivate a deep sense of inner peace and harmony. His message was one of unity and interconnectedness, reminding us that we are all part of a greater whole.

The Impact of Mentorship on Personal Transformation

Wayne Dyer's mentorship has profoundly impacted personal transformation for many across the globe. His teachings have empowered people to break free from their limitations, embrace their true potential, and live with purpose and intention. By offering a blend of spiritual wisdom and practical advice, Dyer provided a roadmap for personal growth that is both inspiring and accessible.

One of the key aspects of Dyer's mentorship was his ability to make complex spiritual concepts understandable and relatable. He had a gift for communicating profound truths in a way that resonated with people from all walks of life. This ability to connect with his audience on a deep level is what made his teachings so impactful and enduring.

Wayne Dyer was a unique and transformative figure in the field of personal development and self-improvement. Several aspects of his approach and personality set him apart from others in the field, making his teachings enduring and impactful. These include:

Authenticity & Relatability

Wayne Dyer's authenticity was one of his most compelling traits. He lived the principles he taught and shared his personal struggles and triumphs with his audience. This openness created a deep connection with his followers, who saw him not just as a teacher but as a fellow traveler on the path of personal growth. His relatability made his teachings more accessible and resonant.

Spiritual Integration

Dyer's ability to integrate spirituality with personal development was a defining characteristic of his work. Unlike many self-help gurus who focused solely on practical strategies for success, Dyer wove spiritual concepts seamlessly into his teachings. He drew from a variety of spiritual traditions, including Taoism, Christianity, and Eastern philosophies, making his message universal and inclusive.

The Power of Intention

Dyer's concept of the power of intention was revolutionary. He taught that intention is a force that shapes our reality, encouraging people to align their intentions with their highest selves. This idea transcended traditional goal setting, positioning intention as a spiritual practice that connects us with the universal energy. This approach resonated deeply with those seeking a more holistic path to personal growth.

Inspirational Storytelling

Wayne Dyer was a master storyteller. He used personal anecdotes, parables, and metaphors to illustrate his points, making complex concepts understandable and relatable. His stories were often imbued with humor and humility, which made his teachings engaging and memorable.

Holistic Approach

Dyer's approach to personal development was holistic, addressing the mind, body, and spirit. He believed in the interconnectedness of all aspects of life and taught that true transformation requires nurturing each of these areas. This holistic perspective appealed to those looking for comprehensive personal growth solutions rather than quick fixes.

Empowerment & Self-Reliance

A central theme in Dyer's teachings was empowerment and self-reliance. He encouraged people to take responsibility for their lives and to recognize their inherent power to create change. His message was one of self-empowerment, teaching that we have the power to shape our destiny through our thoughts, beliefs, and actions.

Focus on Inner Peace & Happiness

While many self-help experts emphasize external success and achievement, Dyer placed a strong emphasis on inner peace and happiness. He taught that true fulfillment comes from within and that external achievements are secondary to inner well-being. This focus on inner peace resonated with those seeking deeper, more meaningful lives.

Inclusivity & Universality

Dyer's teachings transcended cultural, religious, and social boundaries. He drew from a wide range of spiritual and philosophical traditions, making his message relevant to people from diverse backgrounds. His universal approach to personal growth made his teachings applicable to a global audience.

Personal Transformation

Dyer's own life story was a testament to personal transformation. From a challenging childhood in orphanages and foster homes to becoming a globally recognized motivational speaker and author, his life embodied the principles he taught. This personal journey added credibility and depth to his teachings.

Enduring Legacy

Wayne Dyer's legacy endures through his extensive body of work, including over forty books, numerous lectures, and audio and video programs. His teachings continue to inspire new generations, and his influence is evident in the work of contemporary personal development leaders.

Compassionate Presence

Dyer's compassionate and loving presence was palpable. He approached his audience with empathy and kindness, creating a safe space for people to explore their vulnerabilities and seek growth. His compassionate approach made his teachings not just instructive but also healing.

Emphasis on Self-Discovery

Dyer emphasized the importance of self-discovery and self-awareness. He believed that by understanding ourselves and our true nature, we can align our lives with our highest purpose. This focus on self-discovery helped people gain clarity and direction in their personal and professional lives.

Encouraging Risk-Taking & Boldness

Wayne Dyer often encouraged his followers to take risks and embrace bold actions. He believed that stepping out of one's comfort zone is essential for growth and transformation. His encouragement to dream big, take bold steps, and trust in the process inspired many to pursue their aspirations fearlessly.

A Visionary for Personal & Global Transformation

Dyer was not only a visionary for personal transformation but also for global change. He believed that individual growth contributes to the collective well-being of society. His vision extended to creating a more conscious, loving, and harmonious world through the empowerment of individuals.

Wayne Dyer's mentorship was a beacon of light for those seeking to transcend their limitations and embrace their true potential. His teachings on the power of intention, overcoming fear, and living with purpose have inspired countless individuals to create meaningful change in their lives. By embodying the principles he taught, Dyer left a lasting legacy that continues to guide and inspire individuals throughout the world today.

DAWNESE OPENSHAW

About Dawnese Openshaw: Dawnese Openshaw is an agent for CHANGE and is a radically authentic transformational leadership and relationship coach. She is also a John Maxwell certified leadership coach, trainer, and speaker in addition to being a published author in *The Principles of David and Goliath* book series and *The Book of Influence* series and has co-authored a book for adoptive moms.

With over 26 years of experience in small business and non-profit organizations, in 2020, Dawnese expanded her coaching to include families which is now her main focus. She teaches emotional intelligence, communication, and relationship building. She combines her passion for leadership and commitment with strengthening families, primarily serving families with teens. Dawnese empowers families to heal individually and together, creating love and harmony in their hearts and home.

She has been married to her husband, Scott, for 28 years and they are the parents of three amazing children (Randy - 25, Thaniel - 24, and Kayden - 19). They grew their family this summer when Randy got married, adding a beautiful daughter-in-law (Mo).

Author's Website: *www.FullyInvestedFamilies.com*

Book Series Website: www.TheBookOfMentors.com

HONORING DR. WAYNE DYER

DONNA MINER

YOU GET TO CHOOSE

When I think of Wayne Dyer, I can't help but smile and feel a sense of peace. So many factors contribute to this feeling: His experiences, his desire to make this world a better place, how he looked for opportunities and shared what he learned, the calm sound of his voice.

When I think of him being a little kid, growing up in and orphanage and foster homes, I can't help but feel instant compassion for his "little boy self.' It certainly put him in the position to go down either the road of resilience, grit, compassion, with the desire to make a positive difference in this world, or chose the opposite, contributing to this already confused world in a negative way.

When I think of Wayne Dyer's contributions to this world, knowing his background I can't help but wonder, what is it that encourages individuals to make the choices we make? What I mean is, as mentioned previously, he made the "choice" to make a positive impact on this world instead of the alternative. This absolutely fascinates me.

It reminds me of a time when I was in Jr. High. I am not sure what happened and do not recall my words to my dad, I just recall walking up the stairs, looking up and him saying to me, "Mi Hita, why would you CHOOSE to have a BAD day when you can CHOOSE to have a GOOD day? When you have a bad day, everyone around you has a bad day; when you have a good day, everyone around you has a good day."

We DO have choices and Wayne Dyer obviously made the choice to IMPACT and become a mentor to thousands of people. I am grateful for the contributions he chose to make and I love that his impact and legacy will live on in his words forever, influencing everyone and anyone who is exposed to them.

So, let's get to it!

"When you're not in harmony with the energy of love, you've moved away from intention and weaken your ability to activate it through the expression of love."
~ Dr. Wayne Dyer

Love

Wayne tells a story of getting off of a bus on his way to give a lecture in Ephesus, Turkey. There were many, many busses. They all stopped for a restroom break and when Wayne was leaving the restroom, standing at the door was a man. He was an older man who was taking off pieces of dirty paper and handing them to the group, expecting a tip. When he went to hand Wayne the paper, Wayne moved away and headed back to the bus.

He went on to explain that when you want to move into this state of divine love, and you want to move toward a state of ego-lessness, there is a sequence that takes place. And the sequence is that, first, you catch yourself with thoughts that do not align with divine love. And the next part of that sequence is that you go back and correct that thought. So, if you notice it, you stop and make the correction and then you start checking your behavior. You realize you behaved rudely or weren't considerate, or maybe you judged. But if you really want to change your subconscious programming and move to this place called divine love, you go back and correct the behavior.

This is exactly what Wayne did during his time in Turkey. He realized he was caught in ego-based, non-compassionate thinking, causing him to make a judgment of the old man in the restroom.

He stopped himself, changed the sequence and he went back. He found that same man. Wayne had a 20 Euro note in his pocket and handed it to the man and thanked him for the courtesy.

He mentioned how it was easy it was to judge the man when seeing him the first time, to think thoughts about the man and his behavior based on Wayne's past experiences. How many of us have done this before? We make assumptions and then our behavior is dictated by those assumptions when we could be totally wrong.

He also mentioned (once being intentional about showing divine love) that he realized he didn't know the man's situation. Who knows? Maybe this is how he feeds his family?

Wayne goes on to point out that we don't have to give everyone on the street money, but we also do not have to judge them. We can also give a silent blessing and move along. He pointed out that, for him, it was important to correct his behavior, reinforcing the desire to divinely love. And that, to come from a place of compassion, we need to love ourselves, forgive ourselves, and be open to miracles.

When I think about his story, I am encouraged to pay attention to my own behavior. How do I treat people? How do I react? Do I pay attention to others and appreciate their lives and perspectives? There are opportunities every day to practice this, to make an impact, and to leave a legacy as Wayne Dyer did.

Unconditional Love & Fear

As I have listened to Wayne's lessons, I want to share a few words from Wayne himself.

Love and God: divine love and essence are the exact same as they are unconditional. You have to have the same love for God that he's always had for us. Through the worst of our days, through the lowest points of our life, this love has always been there. It's available to us. We can take it anytime. It's never turned away and its supply is inexhaustible. We can't exhaust it. We can't make it go away. It is there.

So, there is a power in unconditional love, and it is very difficult for most of us to grasp. Have you ever been around a person who lives and experiences unconditional love? Because when you are around that person, you discover that the energy that they radiate is infectious. It's like being there with Mother Teresa, just being in her presence.

They said this of Jesus. They said it when they would go into the village, just his presence in the village, nothing more, would change the consciousness of those around. Wow! Can you imagine if we were all intentional with our love and unconditionally loving everyone around us? Not being attached to other people's thoughts, perspectives, actions and just loving them anyway?

This takes me back to another experience I had with my dad. When moving to a new state and being treated like I didn't belong, my dad would tell me, "Mi Hita, love them anyway." I am so grateful for the wisdom that was passed down from a World War II infantry rifleman and have continued to hear his voice, apply his lessons, and share them whenever possible.

So, on the thought of LOVE, I challenge you to an exercise. Wayne mentions this in one of his talks and I love it! Ready? Okay, here we go.

For three days, focus on loving a child, a coworker, friend, spouse, parent etc., and decide that everything you're going to direct to that person is unconditional love—no matter how crappy they may act or no matter how much you may find them to be irritating or whatever. You are going to respond with unconditional love. With the absence of judgment, the absence of anger, the absence of ego, etc…You catch my drift. Let go of everything unconditional love is not.

Try this for three days—unconditional love—and pay attention to what happens in your life, and to notice how you're feeling, how others are treating you, how you are sleeping and what is happening to your dreams. I bet after three days you won't want to stop.

It's astounding how powerful unconditional love is. I would also challenge you to take it one step further: SHARE! Share your experience with as many people that will listen. What a great opportunity to be a part of the growth of others and the knowledge that you have impacted even MORE lives! I love this so much!

Love & Fear

This is pretty cool stuff. Here are just a couple of examples Wayne gives us on how love and fear cannot exist together that I think we can all apply, and, if we are intentional, apply them to many more areas of our lives.

If we are on the freeway, do we drive the speed limit because we fear a ticket? Or do we drive the speed limit because we LOVE that it makes us safer?

Do you eat the foods you eat because are afraid of getting sick if you don't, or do you eat the foods you eat because you LOVE your body?

I could go on and on with examples, but I challenge you to come up with your own, but don't just come up with them. Use and share!

I think if we "flip the switch" and ask ourselves how we can redefine, restate, and we do it with love, we will be in the position to watch our lives change for the better, enabling us to live better quality lives while leaving an impact on others.

And at the end of the day… isn't that what it is all about?

I am going to finish my chapter with a few quotes by Wayne Dyer. I encourage you to not just read them, but to really think about them and how they can apply to your life and assist you in your personal growth journey.

"Give love and unconditional acceptance to those you encounter, and notice what happens."

"Each time you send love in response to hate, you diffuse the hate."

HONORING DR. WAYNE DYER

"There are only two emotions—Fear and Love. Go with Love."

"Whatever the question, love is the answer."

"Loving others starts with loving myself."

"With everything that has happened to you, you can either feel sorry for yourself or treat what has happened as a gift. Everything is either an opportunity to grow or an obstacle to keep you from growing.
YOU get to choose."

~ Dr. Wayne Dyer

DONNA MINER

About Donna Miner: Donna Miner is a seasoned Account Representative with over 25 years of experience in the real estate industry. Since 1996, she has been a pivotal figure in the sector, showcasing her expertise in sales and her dedication to fostering long-lasting relationships. Donna's passion lies in being an integral part of others' success, taking immense pride in witnessing her clients' personal and professional growth. Her professional journey began at U.S. Title, where she served as a Licensed Escrow Officer in 1996. Donna then transitioned to First American Title Company, where she held dual roles as an Account Executive and Licensed Escrow Officer for over 12 years. Since 2012, Donna has been a Sales Executive at Old Republic Title, located in Clearfield, Utah.

Donna has been the recipient of several prestigious awards, including the Presidents Award by Old Republic Title Central Division in 2022 and the $1,000,000 Producer Award for 2021. Additionally, the Northern Wasatch Board of Realtors honored her with the Presidential Achievement Award in 2021. Earlier in her career, while associated with First American Title Company, she was recognized as the Member of the Year by the Northern Wasatch Women's Council of Realtors in 2011 as well as Affiliate of the Year presented by the Weber-North Davis Board of Realtors in 2004 and 2006. Beyond her professional achievements, Donna is actively involved with committees associated with the Northern Wasatch Board of Realtors as an affiliate and maintains her escrow license. Donna spent many years singing in a band and is now a Sales Representative for a national title company. Her journey has also led her to become a certified Sales Mindset Coach under Jay Shetty's guidance. Her true sanctuaries are found on her patio and the beach, and her most cherished bonds are with her family and close friends.

Book Series Website: *www.TheBookOfMentors.com*

HONORING DR. WAYNE DYER

"ABUNDANCE IS NOT SOMETHING WE ACQUIRE. IT IS SOMETHING WE TUNE INTO."

~ DR. WAYNE DYER

EILEEN E. GALBRAITH

INSPIRED TO GREATNESS

Dr. Wayne Dyer, a luminary in the realm of self-improvement, exemplifies the profound truth that the proof of our beliefs lies in the actions we take. His wisdom resonated deeply with me as I embarked on my own journey of personal growth. Dyer's teachings illuminated the power of our thoughts to shape our beliefs, and how our actions and intentions toward those beliefs can catalyze remarkable transformations in our lives.

The proof is in the actions we take. This simple yet profound insight underscores the importance of aligning our thoughts, beliefs, and actions to manifest the life we desire. Through his words and deeds, Dr. Wayne Dyer remains an inspiring figure, reminding us that true transformation begins with the choices we make and the actions we take.

"Go for it now. The future is promised to no one."

This quote encapsulates the essence of seizing the moment, being driven by inspiration, and taking action toward one's goals and aspirations. It encourages individuals to embrace their potential and pursue greatness without hesitation, recognizing that the present moment is the only certainty we have.

"Stop acting as if life is a rehearsal.
Live this day as if it were your last.
The past is over and gone.
The future is not guaranteed."

This quote urges individuals to live fully in the present moment, embracing each day with passion, purpose, and enthusiasm. It emphasizes the importance of making the most of every opportunity and cherishing the precious gift of life. By letting go of regrets about the past and worries about the future, we can truly be inspired to greatness in the here and now.

The depth of wisdom emanating from this individual is profound, considering his humble beginnings as an orphan, abandoned by his father when he was just a toddler. Born in the 1940s, one can only speculate on the potential trajectory of his life had he not made the conscious decision to redirect its course.

Dr. Dyer's prolific literary output, comprising over forty books, has served as a wellspring of inspiration for countless individuals, me included. My initial introduction to his work dates to the early 2000s. As a perpetual student of personal development and an inherently curious individual, I vividly recall receiving a copy of one of his books from one of my managers. Delving into his teachings not only reaffirmed my existing beliefs but also empowered me to cultivate greater resilience and strength in my personal journey.

You might be curious about my most significant insight. In three succinct words: "Thoughts are things." Consider this: every creation in the world originates twice—first in the realm of thought, as someone conceives a solution to a challenge, and then in reality, as that solution materializes.

Imagine the human mind as a powerful generator, capable of conceiving and manifesting ideas into tangible reality. Every invention, every innovation, every creation that has ever graced the world first began as a mere thought in someone's mind. Whether it's the towering skyscrapers that punctuate city skylines, the intricate technologies that shape our daily lives, or the stirring works of art that evoke deep emotions, they all originated from the fertile soil of human imagination.

Consider, for instance, the invention of the light bulb by Thomas Edison. Before the first flicker of electric light illuminated the darkness, it existed as a vision in Edison's mind—a relentless pursuit sparked by the thought that there must be a better way to illuminate the world. Through experimentation, perseverance, and unwavering belief in his idea, Edison transformed that initial thought, with the assistance of many workers, into a tangible reality that revolutionized human existence. He had the thought; the team created the reality.

Similarly, the words we speak, the actions we take, and the decisions we make are all rooted in the thoughts that occupy our minds. Whether positive or negative, our thoughts possess a remarkable creative power—they shape our perceptions, influence our behaviors, and ultimately determine the course of our lives.

Given that thoughts possess the power to shape our reality, let's delve into the significance of the words we think and speak. Every syllable, every sound resonates within us, making its way through our ears and into the depths of our subconscious mind. Whether consciously acknowledged or not, we are actively crafting our reality, as our subconscious absorbs not only the words we utter but also the tone in which we express them.

Certain individuals categorize these thoughts as our limiting beliefs when they tend toward negativity, while they consider them our inherent beliefs when we genuinely perceive them as truths.

How does our mind discern between these classifications? What evidence exists to differentiate a negative thought from a positive one, and how does this distinction influence our subsequent actions and intentions regarding that belief?

Here are some potential contrasts between negative and positive aspects:

Emotional Response: Our mind discerns between negative and positive thoughts based on the emotional response they evoke. Negative thoughts typically trigger feelings of fear, doubt, or anxiety, while positive thoughts elicit emotions such as joy, confidence, or hope.

Physical Sensations: Negative thoughts may manifest as physical sensations of tension, discomfort, or unease in the body, signaling their adverse effects. In contrast, positive thoughts often correspond with sensations of relaxation, warmth, or energy.

Behavioral Patterns: Our past experiences and learned behaviors shape our perception of thoughts as negative or positive. If a thought aligns with patterns of self-doubt or pessimism, it's likely deemed negative, whereas thoughts consistent with optimism and self-assurance are considered positive.

Impact on Well-Being: Negative thoughts tend to erode our mental and emotional well-being, leading to stress, depression, or low self-esteem. Conversely, positive thoughts contribute to enhanced resilience, optimism, and overall life satisfaction.

Influence on Actions & Intentions: The distinction between negative and positive thoughts profoundly influences our subsequent actions and intentions. Negative thoughts often breed inertia, avoidance, or self-sabotage, limiting our potential and hindering progress. In contrast, positive thoughts inspire proactive behavior, resilience in the face of challenges, and a greater alignment with our goals and aspirations.

In essence, "thoughts are things" serves as a potent reminder of the profound influence our thoughts wield over our reality. By harnessing the creative power of our minds, we possess the ability to shape our destiny, manifest our aspirations, and contribute to the collective tapestry of human experience. As we cultivate a mindset of clarity, intentionality, and possibility, we unlock the boundless potential that resides within us, propelling us toward the realization of our deepest dreams and aspirations.

In summary, this is titled "Inspired to Greatness" because it dives into the profound influence of thoughts on our journey toward personal fulfillment and success. It explores how our minds discern between negative and positive thoughts, considering emotional responses, physical sensations, behavioral patterns, and their impact on overall well-being.

Negative thoughts, often characterized by fear, doubt, and tension, hinder progress and limit potential. Conversely, positive thoughts evoke feelings of joy, confidence, and relaxation, inspiring proactive behavior, and resilience in the face of challenges.

This writing highlights the transformative power of aligning our thoughts with our aspirations. By cultivating optimism and self-assurance, individuals can overcome obstacles and pursue their goals with unwavering determination. Through introspection and self-awareness, we can recognize and challenge limiting beliefs, redirecting our focus toward possibilities and opportunities for growth.

Ultimately, by harnessing the creative potential of our minds and embracing a mindset of possibility, we can unlock our inherent greatness and embark on a path of purpose and fulfillment.

Dr. Wayne Dyer departed from this world in 2015, yet his legacy continues to resonate across generations. Personally impacted by his teachings, the profound influence of his work remains palpable for this writer. It serves as a poignant reminder of the power inherent in our words, as our minds absorb and respond to them.

With mindfulness, we recognize the significance of our thoughts, speaking with intention, and aligning our actions with our beliefs. Through this intentional practice, we unveil our true potential and manifest the reality we are destined to inhabit.

EILEEN E. GALBRAITH

About Eileen E Galbraith: Throughout her journey, mentors consistently hailed Eileen's joy in service, her intuitive grasp of people's desires, and her aversion to conventional sales tactics. For Eileen, sales were never about coercion; they were about understanding needs and offering solutions with sincerity and empathy.

However, it was adversity that propelled Eileen into the realm of entrepreneurship. Confronting personal crises, she discovered a reservoir of resilience and empathy within herself, prompting her to extend counsel to other women facing similar challenges. Thus, her accidental foray into entrepreneurship birthed two ventures in the early 2000s, now united under a single banner.

Today, Eileen is not just a sought-after speaker and multi-time Amazon Bestselling author; she is the visionary behind "Implement to Impact," a coaching enterprise dedicated to empowering women entrepreneurs. With a focus on fostering time freedom, wealth creation, and a supportive community, Eileen's mission resonates deeply with those she serves, embodying the transformative power of empowerment. Learn more about Eileen at: *www.RenewedAbundance.com.*

Author's Website: *www.ImplementToImpact.com*

Book Series Website: *www.TheBookOfMentors.com*

ERIC D. JACKSON

MISSED MENTORSHIP: NATURE & ITS PRINCIPLES ARE A GOOD MENTOR

"Security is an imagination. Nothing in nature is secure."
~ **Dr. Wayne Dyer**

And yet, Wayne Dyer wrote, "Every goal is possible from here... You can find The Great Way by closely studying nature."

Calls to Action from Personal Values Toward Mentorship

I chose Wayne Dyer's book, *Change Your Thoughts - Change Your Life: Living the Wisdom of the Tao,* as my reference for this chapter because of its focus on nature, and we can learn so many lessons from nature!

"The journey of a thousand miles begins with a single step."
~ Lao Tsu, the Tao

Cheers! Here's to the next steps in your journey!

In this four-part series of *The Book of Mentors*, my concept for this series could not have worked out any better than to have this chapter highlight Wayne Dyer's work by emphasizing "Nature's Principles" as a good mentor for us.

You can read about "Reverse Mentorship" with "Crisis" as teacher in our Zig Ziglar edition, and "Negative Mentorship" with "Science" as teacher in our Bob Proctor edition. And if you want a sneak peek... the fourth for my series in these contributions will be "Mind the Mentorship Gaps" with "Life" as our teacher.

All of these have been designed to offer a counter point of view because life does not always go according to plan, and to let you know it can be okay when it does not. You can adapt—you can still have hope, and a plan, and you can take positive action toward living the fullest expression of your life!

"You can re-calibrate your caliber in any moment."
~ Eric D. Jackson

I looked up the definition of the word 'principle,' and it generally means 'first steps' or 'origins,' the 'foundation' or 'elements' from which "the fundamental tenets or doctrines of a system, a law or truth on which others are founded."

When you commit yourself to personal and professional growth, and read Dyer's works, or the varied authors contributing to the books in this series of Mentors (or any other works throughout history for that matter), I want to offer two things for you to always consider:

1. Keep in mind that we are all human and imperfect.

2. Always seek to understand the foundations of what any person is sharing with you as your mentor and guide.

Test any principles to discover what they are founded on and how often they are true. A Law should be true all the time, every time. A principle should prove true most of the time, in most situations. They should be trustworthy and reliable for you, even when people and circumstances let you down.

"See God everywhere; make it a daily practice to see the invisible force of God in everything you see and hear."
~ Dr. Wayne Dyer

There are varied disciplines and perspectives that you can draw wisdom and inspiration from, and they display their principles all around you for your benefit and application if you choose to learn from them and put them into good use. That's why each of my contributions spotlight a different aspect to learn from when things aren't perfect.

People are imperfect. As the quote from Wayne Dyer above states, "Nothing in nature is secure."

I usually say it this way: "We live in an imperfect world, with imperfect people making imperfect decisions, getting imperfect results."

This is especially true when it comes to let downs and missed opportunities you may have encountered in your own journey so far. Sometimes a mentor seems absent or does not 'appear' in our journey. And, sometimes, a person may not be a good fit or be aware of what being a good mentor could be—either way, this results in Missed Mentorship.

This is why giving ourselves and others Grace is one of the secrets or keys to this life. Another secret to life and decoding other truths is seeing everything and answering life's mysteries through the lens of what a positive, healthy relationship would look like.

When you are evaluating a Law or a Principle and how true it is, can the rich essence of a thing be unlocked by evaluating it through the lens of a caring, loving, and healthy relationship? Life is about people, so the truths of this life together should prove to be true through healthy relationships.

Try it. Test it and see if this doesn't start to expand your understanding of a better world and a better long-term future. This can be a challenge if we have had unhealthy patterns modeled for us, but if we envision and choose what a healthy version of life will be for us, we can begin to grow in our application of life's mentoring laws and principles.

My goal is never to push my own beliefs or philosophies on you or any person, but to invite you to step into your own journey and explore life's principles for yourself in a way that has meaningful and lasting impact for you personally. Test everything.

Another way to test and uncover truths is to hold tension, or to weigh the space between paradoxes and dichotomies. Wayne Dyer spends a good portion spotlighting from the Tao many examples of nature, showing us truths between opposing things.

According to Wayne Dyer, "ALL depends on opposites," and yet, "ALL is perfect in oneness... Allow duality while seeing unity (Yin/Yang)."

I want to offer you an opportunity to not see tension as a negative or a stressor, but to see it actually as balance or harmony. We get stressed when we pull or lean into one area while neglecting another. Paradoxes and dichotomies can help us visualize points that hold tension in balance for us, and maybe we might be able to find more truth in the middle. Try it.

For the fullness of your potential, AND all your imperfection, find a humble and empowering set of perspectives. Taking from the Tao, living from greatness begins with knowing "...you are pure greatness...." Wayne Dyer continued, "See the unfolding of God in all that you encounter. You will become more like him, and less like that which tarnished your link to him."

Sometimes we might be tempted to take the philosophies of greatness, meant to inspire us, out of context and/or out of balance with us also being human, fallible, and mortal. Robin Williams played the part of an animated Genie in the story of "Aladdin" and perfectly referenced that being a Genie had its limitations and rules: "Phenomenal cosmic power, itty bitty living space!"

Whoever you are being mentored by, and whatever influences you may choose in your life, I hope that you would consider this chapter, and seek to learn and apply the timeless wisdom and principles that will guide you toward your fullest potential, and most humble and empowering perspectives so that you can live out your purpose and make a difference in the lives you impact and serve.

Change Your Thoughts, Change Your Life.

Each of Wayne Dyer's chapter essay titles begins with, "Living By (or In, or With) _____." How are you 'Living (by/in/with)' in each area of life and work that is important to you? How do you want to be Living? What do you need to change and take those first steps toward your new and improved future?

Here are some values (in each book of the series) that you can take into your mentorship opportunities that will serve you well:

- Accountability
- Humility to Learn
- Responsiveness
- Multiplication

Accountability

Wayne Dyer concludes each verse of the Tao, and offers his next steps: "Do the Tao now." I want you to evaluate what you are learning from your mentor and life's principles and ask yourself what you are willing to be accountable for as your next action steps. What can and WILL you do in the next 24 to 36 hours? Be willing to report back to your mentor the actions you took and the results/feedback you got for future review and improvement.

Humility

"Seek the way of water," or be humble to take the path that flows and is flexible. Being humble is to be flexible. It also allows you the ability to gain new insights, learning, and perspective. Humility positions you, as you step back calmly into it, to enter into the flow of powerful emotions and awareness of your environment, beliefs, and values so that when you speak and act, you are in alignment with all that matters to you.

Responsiveness

In your willingness to respond to the different relationships and environments around you, look for opportunities to respond (or live) harmoniously with the laws and principles of life and nature. What have you learned, are you learning, or can you learn as you practice and test these principles in real-life situations?

"Embrace transformation" in order "to fulfill one's destiny...to be constant." Or, the only constant is change! Embrace it and respond from a place of constant application of principles that are proving to yield positive and consistent results in your life.

Multiplication (Living by Offering the Surplus - The Tao)

"Only a man or woman of the Tao, or God, can give to others without taking... Be an instrument of increasing where you see deficiencies (money, time, compassion, love, joy, forgiveness)."
~ Dr. Wayne Dyer

Giving without taking—isn't that the impression you have of what good mentoring actually is? As you receive and learn from your mentors and from the laws of nature, receive them with an abundant and generous mindset. Become an instrument of increase to those around you. Multiply what you receive from mentoring and offer it to others in a way that equips them also to go and multiply it in others also.

"I am responsible for choosing the way I see things - I choose the feelings I experience."
~ Dr. Wayne Dyer

ERIC D. JACKSON

About Eric D. Jackson: Eric Jackson has led high-performance teams for leading organizations in marketing and financial sectors and helped clients from family-owned to Fortune 100 companies achieve their desired results. He is the founder of Transformational Leadership & Culture International, and Jackson Insurance and Financial Services.

As a Champion of People, Leadership and Culture Eric loves helping people create transformation in what matters most to them, and for their people so they can grow their influence, team, and impact. He helps leaders to GAIN, RETAIN, and TRAIN for high performance results for themselves and for their teams to create breakthrough and take practical action steps toward growth and improvement.

Eric is a certified leadership coach, trainer, and speaker with the Maxwell Leadership Team, and with SCALE Architects and the Predictable Success model. As a speaker, trainer and coach he is also a practitioner in his own life and businesses. He has studied people and leadership since he was in grade school, always driven to find a better way, and to share what he has learned with people so they too can create their own desired life transformations.

In his free time Eric enjoys playing golf, and volunteering with youth leadership programs. Eric is passionate about helping others to make a difference in their lives and the world we live in.

Author's Website: *ItsYourLif.com/Books*

Book Series Website: *www.TheBookOfMentors*

HONORING DR. WAYNE DYER

FRED MOSKOWITZ

FOCUS MORE ON ENJOYING YOUR JOURNEY

Focus More on Enjoying Your Journey Than Focusing Solely on Your Destination

Without any hesitation, I will share with you that one of the most impactful lessons I have learned from the teachings of Dr. Wayne Dyer may be summed up in one of his most iconic quotes: *"Be open to everything and attached to nothing."*

Any time that we are working on a project, goal, or objective, it is likely that we will experience a very bumpy road, full of many highs and many lows. In this journey of life, I have found that the trajectory is never smooth, and we are presented with many opportunities to learn and develop ourselves throughout the process. Through employing healthy amounts of curiosity, a desire to learn, and by applying persistence, we are offered a unique opportunity to enjoy the journey that we are on in pursuit of our goals.

Handling Our Emotions

Have you ever experienced a time when you became so attached to a particular outcome that you were completely consumed by your own thoughts and emotions? The outcome could be small or large, such as scoring well on a test, landing a new job, completing a business deal, or even asking someone out on a date. Oftentimes, it becomes extremely easy to focus only on the final outcome, while we neglect to enjoy the journey that we are on, in pursuit of that outcome.

Let's consider the idea that any time we become attached to a particular outcome, it is possible that we might experience some negative emotions such as failure and disappointment. How many times has it happened that things did not work out exactly the way you had planned? As best as we might try, it is impossible to control the entire universe. Life can sometimes serve us rather healthy portions of randomness and unpredictability. And, when we become very attached to a specific outcome, we become closed to other opportunities and possibilities, effectively shutting them down abruptly as we have become unadaptable and rigid.

While we are on the journey, think about the richness of the experience; think about the possibilities. We might be learning and developing some valuable skills. We might be meeting new people and building the start of some great relationships. We might be experiencing personal growth and self-development. We might be serving someone else and adding value to others. These are all things that enrich our lives and help us to become a better version of ourselves.

Getting into the Energy of Curiosity

When we talk about curiosity, let's observe the best role models and demonstrators of curiosity: Children. Think about the last time that you interacted with young children. What are they like? They are all about exploring, playing, asking questions, and testing theories. Any time that I watch children in action (think about a baby learning to walk), the pattern that I see is all about failing fast, adapting and making changes, and then reiterating with a new approach.

When I was working as a computer engineer in the tech industry, I worked at several companies that utilized what is known as the agile software development model. The basic premise of this model is to employ a collaborative effort to define product requirements, create a functional product, perform testing and discovery, respond to change, ship the product, retrospectively review progress, and work deliverables. And then, go back and repeat the entire process again and again.

Throughout this process, a high value was placed on failing fast and failing often. Along the way, course corrections and fixes were quickly implemented, resulting in a product that was continuously evolving and improving over time.

Striving to be a Lifelong Learner

Some people make an unfortunate mistake in shutting themselves down to all learning once they graduate from school. I recently read a statistic that shared some rather unfortunate news, in that 33% of high school graduates never read another book after high school graduation and 42% of college grads never read another book after college.

We have diverse ways available for us to learn. All it takes is setting an intention and then taking action. There is certainly no shortage of opportunities and resources that are available to us. We have books, audiobooks, podcasts, streaming videos, online courses and programs, online summits, seminars, and in-person workshops and classes.

Learning in this fashion takes hard work and effort. We will need to invest both time and money into our learning. And, like many other habits, when we apply a persistent and consistent focus over a longer duration of time, the results begin to compound and grow.

Getting Comfortable with Being Uncomfortable

In the psychological community, the concept of the four zones has been established. These are known as the Comfort Zone, Fear Zone, Learning Zone, and Growth Zone.

Most of us are familiar with the concept of being in the comfort zone. When we are in our comfort zone, we are functioning in an area where there is minimal risk and a high degree of certainty about our outcomes. We feel safe and we are met with little or no challenges. Another characteristic of the comfort zone is that there is a very low incentive to achieve a higher level of performance and results. The comfort zone is where people do what they've always done, and as a result they get what they've always gotten.

When we start to progress beyond the outer limits of our comfort zone, we begin to enter the fear zone. In the fear zone, the emotions of fear and discomfort tend to show up. There are very specific thought patterns that can appear, and these include being easily influenced by others' opinions, not trusting oneself, and making excuses to stop and retreat to the comfort zone.

After pushing through the fear zone, we then enter the learning zone. In the learning zone, this is where we begin to acquire new skills and creative solutions, and to experience our own growth. We find ways to handle challenges successfully. We become resourceful and creative, and we begin to see results.

Beyond the learning zone, we start to experience the growth zone. This is a glorious place to be, and it can certainly feel like the pinnacle of achievement. Here, we acknowledge and recognize our achievements, and we start to think about setting new and even higher goals.

As a relatable case study, think back to a time when you (or it could be someone close to you) were learning to ride a bicycle. Remember the feelings and emotions you felt during that first time that you sat on the bicycle seat and you placed your feet solidly on the ground to support yourself. This is what it is like to be in the comfort zone.

Progressing on to the fear zone, I invite you to recall how it felt when you lifted your feet off the ground and attempted to put them on the pedals. How did it feel when the bicycle started to lean or tilt to one side? Maybe you took some risk and even started to move forward, and the bicycle became wobbly and unstable. For most people, the instinctual reaction is to immediately place your feet back on the ground to support oneself, back to stability, safety, and certainty.

It could take several attempts of this, perhaps a couple of failures and falls to the ground. Imagine yourself pushing harder and getting some momentum so that the bicycle is rolling forward. You push on the pedals to generate more forward motion, and you can feel that the bicycle picks up more and more stability. Perhaps you experience another fall; however, you pick yourself up, and you are happy that you moved forward by a couple of feet. This progress motivates you further and you make more and more attempts. You are learning and you are figuring this out. You might be a little beat up and bruised—but welcome to the learning zone!

And finally, you have reached a glorious breakthrough. You are gaining even more skill; you are now able to get the bicycle moving steadily. You figure out the brakes and steering the handlebars. You have gained the confidence that when you are moving forward, you can control the bicycle and the momentum with increasing grace and stability. You now start to think about covering longer distances (setting new goals). With more and more practice, you soon develop the ability to ride the bicycle without thinking about it. Perhaps you become intrigued with starting to think about the idea of learning how to ride a unicycle. This is what it feels like to be in the growth zone.

Final Thoughts

Throughout this chapter, we have learned that life is an amazing and fantastic journey. And, if we are fully present throughout that journey, we get to enjoy and benefit from all of the richness, the excitement, the fulfillment, and the personal growth that is offered to us. I invite you to savor the beauty of living in the moment!

When we become intentional about handling our emotions, getting into the energy of curiosity, the pursuit of lifelong learning, and constantly pushing to get into the edge of our comfort zones, the result is that we begin to show up in life playing at a higher level.

May the rich philosophies of Dr. Wayne Dyer continue to live on in all your daily lives.

FRED MOSKOWITZ

About Fred Moskowitz: Fred Moskowitz is a Bestselling Author, investment fund manager, and speaker who is on a personal mission to teach people about the power of investing in alternative asset classes, such as real estate and mortgage notes, showing them the way to diversify their capital into investments that are uncorrelated from Wall Street and the stock markets.

Through his body of work, he is teaching investors the strategies to build passive income and cash flow streams designed to flow into their bank accounts. He's a frequent event speaker and contributor to investment podcasts.

Fred is the author of *The Little Green Book of Note Investing: A Practical Guide for Getting Started with Investing in Mortgage Notes* and contributing author in *1Habit To Thrive in a Post-Covid World.*

Author's Website: *www.FredMoskowitz.com*

Book Series Website: *www.TheBookOfMentors.com*

JEFFREY LEVINE

MENTORSHIP & THE POWER OF PURPOSE

The concept of mentorship has always been a driving force in my life. From my early years at Albany Academy to my time at the University of Hartford, to the University of Mississippi Law School, and then to Boston University School of Law, mentorship has been the cornerstone of my personal and professional growth. I am reminded of the words of Dr. Wayne Dyer: "When you change the way you look at things, the things you look at change." This profound truth has guided me through every stage of my life and continues to influence the way I mentor others today.

A Foundation Built on Mentorship

My introduction to mentorship began in the classrooms of Albany Academy, where I was fortunate to encounter teachers who saw potential in me and nurtured my thirst for knowledge. These early experiences laid the foundation for my future endeavors, teaching me the importance of guidance, support, and the power of belief. The lessons I learned from my mentors were not just academic; they were life lessons that shaped my character and instilled in me a deep-seated commitment to giving back.

As I moved through the halls of the University of Hartford, the University of Mississippi Law School, and the Boston University School of Law, this commitment to mentorship only deepened. I realized that mentorship was not just about imparting knowledge but about inspiring others to reach their full potential. It was about helping others see the possibilities within themselves and guiding them on a path to success.

One of the most significant moments in my career came when I realized the power of paradigms, a concept introduced to me by Bob Proctor— you can read and learn more about this in great depth by reading my chapter contribution and all the amazing co-authors' chapters in volume 2 of this series, *The Book of Mentors, Honoring Legacy Legend Bob Proctor.* Paradigms, as Bob explained, are mental programs that control our habitual behavior, often keeping us stuck in patterns of thought and action that limit our potential. Understanding this concept was a turning point in my life, allowing me to break free from the limitations that had held me back and embrace a mindset of growth and possibility.

The Power of Paradigms

In my career as a financial planner and tax attorney, I encountered countless individuals who were held back by their paradigms. They had the desire to succeed, but their mental programming kept them from taking the necessary steps to achieve their goals. This realization led me to become a Mindset Money Mentor, helping my clients overcome their limiting beliefs and empowering them to take control of their financial future.

One of the most powerful tools I use in my mentorship is the "Impression of Increase," a concept that Bob Proctor emphasized throughout his teachings. The idea is simple: always leave people with the impression of increase. This means that every interaction should leave the other person feeling better, more empowered, and more capable of achieving their goals. It is a philosophy that I have embraced in all aspects of my life, from my work with clients to my relationships with family and friends.

Dr. Wayne Dyer once said, "You cannot always control what goes on outside, but you can always control what goes on inside." This quote perfectly encapsulates the essence of the Impression of Increase. It is about cultivating a positive mindset, regardless of external circumstances, and using that mindset to uplift and inspire others.

Mentorship in Action

As I reflect on my journey in mentorship, I am reminded of the countless lives I have had the privilege of touching and influencing both in the financial world and as well as in the coaching and mindset realm. One of the most rewarding aspects of mentorship is seeing the transformation in those I have guided. It is a humbling experience to watch someone overcome their limiting beliefs, embrace their potential, and achieve their dreams.

One of the most memorable examples of this transformation came from a client who had been struggling with self-doubt for years. She had the skills and knowledge to succeed, but her paradigm kept telling her that she wasn't good enough. Through our work together, she was able to break free from this limiting belief and embrace a new mindset of possibility. Today, she is thriving in her career and living a life of fulfillment and purpose.

This is the true power of mentorship: the ability to help others see the possibilities within themselves and guide them on a path to success. It's a selfless act of serving other and imparting knowledge, experience, and confidence on those seeking greater results in their lives. It is a responsibility that I do not take lightly, and it is a role that I am honored to fulfill.

The Importance of Purpose

As I continue to mentor others, I am increasingly aware of the importance of purpose. Purpose is the driving force behind everything we do, and it is what gives our lives meaning and direction. Without purpose, we are like ships adrift at sea, without a clear destination or a sense of direction.

One of the most powerful quotes from Dr. Wayne Dyer is, "When you stay on purpose and refuse to be discouraged by fear, you align with the infinite self, in which all possibilities exist." This quote speaks to the importance of staying true to our purpose, even in the face of challenges and setbacks. It is a reminder that when we align with our purpose, we tap into a source of infinite potential and possibility.

In my work as a mentor, I strive to help others discover their purpose and align their lives with that purpose. Whether it is guiding a client through the complexities of financial planning or helping someone overcome their limiting beliefs, my goal is always to help them connect with their true purpose and live a life of meaning and fulfillment.

The Future of Mentorship

I am excited about the possibilities that lie ahead. I believe that mentorship is more important now than ever before, as we navigate a world that is increasingly complex and uncertain. In this ever-changing landscape, the guidance and support of a mentor can be the difference between success and failure, between living a life of purpose and merely existing.

I am committed to continuing my work as a mentor, helping others overcome their limiting beliefs, discover their purpose, and achieve their full potential. I believe that we all have a responsibility to give back, to share our knowledge and experiences with others, and to help them on their journey to success.

In the words of Dr. Wayne Dyer, "The highest form of ignorance is when you reject something you don't know anything about." This quote serves as a reminder to remain open to new ideas, to continue learning and growing, and to always be willing to share that knowledge with others.

A Legacy of Mentorship

I am filled with gratitude for the mentors who have guided me, the clients who have trusted me, and the opportunities I have had to make a difference in the lives of others. I am proud of the legacy I have built, but I am even more excited about the future and the possibilities that lie ahead.

Mentorship is not just a role; it is a calling. It is a responsibility to guide, uplift, and inspire others. It is a legacy that transcends wealth and status, a gift that is measured in the lives we touch and the positive change we create.

I am committed to continuing this journey, embracing the future with positivity and purpose, and leaving a legacy of empowerment, inspiration, and positive change. This is the power of mentorship, and this is the legacy I am honored to leave behind.

Dr. Wayne Dyer once said, "The only limits you have are the limits you believe." This quote is a powerful reminder that our potential is limitless, and it is up to us to unlock that potential and achieve greatness.

As I continue on this path of mentorship, I am committed to helping others break free from their limiting beliefs, discover their true potential, and live a life of purpose and fulfillment. Together, we can create a brighter, more empowered future for all.

JEFFREY LEVINE

About Jeffrey Levine: Jeffrey is a highly skilled tax planner and business strategist, as well as a published author and sought-after speaker. He's been featured in national magazines, on the cover of *Influential People Magazine*, and is a frequent featured expert on radio, talk shows, and documentaries. Jeffrey attended the prestigious Albany Academy for high school and then went on to the University of Hartford at Connecticut, the University of Mississippi Law School, and Boston University School of Law, and earned an L.L.M. in taxation. His accolades include features in Kiplinger and Family Circle Magazine, as well as a dedicated commentator for Channel 6 and 13 news shows, a contributor for the *Albany Business Review*, and a talk show host for WGY Radio.

Jeffrey has accumulated more than 30 years of experience as a tax attorney and certified financial planner and has given in excess of 500 speeches nationally. Levine is the executive producer and cast member in the documentary *Beyond the Secret: The Awakening*.

Levine's most current work, Consistent Profitable Growth Map, is a step-by-step workbook outlining easy-to-follow steps to convert consistent revenue growth to any business platform.

Author's Website: *www.Strategies.org*

Book Series Website: *www.TheBookOfMentors.com*

"DO NOT DIE WITH YOUR MUSIC STILL IN YOU."

~ DR. WAYNE DYER

HONORING DR. WAYNE DYER

JON KOVACH JR.

THE LAW OF DIVINE ONENESS

"Go for it now. The future is promised to no one."
~ Dr. Wayne Dyer

For as long as I can remember, I have felt an interconnectedness with people and my environment. It feels like one thread connecting us all—a thread of unity, compassion, and shared existence. I believe that thread is one of many laws and principles taught by Dr. Wayne W. Dyer, who referred to this principle as the "Law of Divine Oneness." This law suggests that every person, place, and thing in the universe is intricately linked. It teaches us that our actions, thoughts, and feelings have significance beyond our immediate surroundings. By recognizing this connection, we can foster a more profound sense of empathy and understanding in our daily lives.

In moments of reflection, I often contemplate how my choices and actions have impacted those around me and the world at large. It's a humbling realization that encourages me to act more intentionally and kindly. Small acts of compassion, a smile, or a helping hand can reverberate in ways we might never fully comprehend. Such pondering also leads me to believe that the greater my personal growth, actions, and development, the greater this world will also grow, achieve, and become.

The Law of Divine Oneness invites all to look beyond superficial differences and appreciate the intrinsic value in every individual. It reminds us that we share much more in common beneath the surface than we might initially perceive.

I strive to live a life that honors the interconnectedness of all things, which is innately the most incredible standard of humanity. Whether through mindful living, nurturing relationships, or advocating for positive change, I am committed to contributing to a world where unity and compassion triumph. I also accept the role of a mentee/lifelong learner who seeks mentorship from others. As a mentee, this law is not just a concept to be understood but a way of life that can profoundly impact our relationships, our growth, and the world at large.

Understanding the Law of Divine Oneness

The Law of Divine Oneness is a fundamental principle that suggests that everything in the universe is interconnected. At the most basic level, we are all made of the same energy and source. This law teaches us that our thoughts, actions, and energies influence not only our lives but also the lives of others and the collective consciousness of the world.

Dr. Wayne Dyer taught that this law cultivates compassion, empathy, and understanding. When we recognize our interconnectedness, it becomes clear that the hurt we inflict on others, intentionally or unintentionally, is the hurt we inflict on ourselves. Conversely, the love, kindness, and generosity we offer to others echo back to us in ways that enrich our lives beyond measure. That also means that all the wins, successes, and achievements we accumulate will mirror their effects and rub off on those in our circles of influence.

In my life, I've experienced the profound impact of this law through the relationships I've built with my mentors and the mentees I've had the privilege to guide. Each relationship, each interaction, is a reflection of this divine affinity. When we approach mentorship as a relationship with the understanding that we are all part of this universe of oneness, the dynamic shifts from hierarchy to mutual growth and respect.

My Journey with Compassionate Mentorship

One of the earliest lessons I learned about mentorship was from my father, who demonstrated the Law of Divine Oneness in the simplest yet most powerful way. As I mentioned in my previous chapters, he would wake my brother and me early on snowy mornings to shovel the driveways of elderly neighbors. It wasn't a chore but an act of service that taught us the importance of caring for others without expecting anything in return. This was one of many learning experiences with the idea that we are all connected and that our personal growth actions influence the lives of others.

My mentors further reinforced this lesson and exemplified compassion in their guidance. They didn't just offer advice; they connected with me on a deeper level, understanding my struggles, fears, and aspirations. One mentor, in particular, always emphasized the importance of truly listening to the needs and concerns of those we seek to help. He taught me that mentorship is not just about imparting knowledge but about understanding the person in front of you as an extension of yourself, deserving of the same love and care you would offer to your own soul.

This approach to mentorship has been a cornerstone of my life and work. Whether I'm coaching a young professional in my networking groups or guiding a colleague through a tough decision, I always strive to see the divine in them—the part of them that is connected to me, to others, and to the universe. This perspective deepens the bond between us and creates an environment where true growth and transformation can occur.

The Role of Empathy in Personal Growth

Empathy is a natural extension of the Law of Divine Oneness. When we understand that we are all connected, it becomes easier to empathize with others and feel their pain, joy, and struggles as our own. Empathy allows us to break down the barriers that separate us and to build bridges of understanding and support.

I have seen firsthand how empathy can transform lives. I recall working with a young entrepreneur who was struggling to find her footing in a competitive industry. She was on the brink of giving up, overwhelmed by self-doubt and the fear of failure. Rather than offering a quick solution or advice, I took the time to listen to her story to understand the emotions behind her words. By doing so, I was able to connect with her on a deeper level, to see the world through her eyes.

This connection allowed me to guide her with practical advice and the emotional support she needed to regain her confidence. Together, we built her self-belief, aligned her goals with her true passions, and created a plan that resonated with her on a soul level. Today, she is thriving, not just in her business but also in her personal life. This experience reinforced my belief that when we approach mentorship with empathy, we empower others to grow in ways they never thought possible.

Building Unity Through Leadership & Mastermind Methodologies

Leadership, in its greatest form, is about bringing people together—uniting them around a common vision, purpose, or goal. The Law of Divine Oneness plays a critical role in this process. When leaders understand that they are not separate from those they lead but rather an integral part of a unified team, they can inspire and motivate others in a way that fosters collaboration and unity.

One of the most powerful tools I continue to use to build unity is mastermind methodologies, concepts deeply rooted in the collective consciousness and shared infinite intelligence principles. Inspired by the teachings of Napoleon Hill in *Think and Grow Rich* and further influenced by mentors and legacy legends like Bob Proctor, the mastermind methodologies leverage the idea that when two or more minds come together in the spirit of harmony with a shared purpose, they create a third, greater mind. This energy is greater than the sum of its parts.

In my experience, mastermind groups are a living manifestation of the Law of Divine Oneness. Each member brings their unique perspectives, experiences, and strengths to the table, contributing to a collective wisdom that benefits everyone involved. Whether it's a group of entrepreneurs brainstorming solutions to business challenges or a team of leaders strategizing for future growth, the synergy created in a mastermind setting is evidence of our interconnectedness.

Through these groups, I have witnessed incredible transformations—not just in business success but in each participant's personal growth and development. The sense of unity and support that emerges from a mastermind group is unparalleled. It is a space where competition is replaced by collaboration, where all celebrate the success of one, and where the group shoulders the challenges of one.

One of my most profound experiences with a mastermind group was during a leadership retreat I facilitated a few years ago. The group consisted of leaders from various industries, each facing unique challenges in their professional lives. As we delved into the mastermind process, it became clear that, despite their differences, they shared everyday struggles—struggles that stemmed from a sense of isolation and the pressure always to have the answers.

Through the mastermind sessions, these leaders began to open up, share their vulnerabilities, and support each other in ways that went beyond the professional realm. They realized that they were not alone in their struggles, that their challenges were not unique, and that they could lean on each other for guidance and strength. By the end of the retreat, they had formed a bond that transcended their professional roles—a bond rooted in the understanding that they were all part of something greater than themselves.

Embrace the Law of Divine Oneness

I am filled with a deep sense of gratitude and purpose over the years of accumulated lessons I have learned from my mentors and the impact of the Law of Divine Oneness on my life. This law has shaped how I approach mentorship and leadership and influenced how I live my life. It has taught me that we are all connected, that our actions have far-reaching consequences, and that we can create a more compassionate, empathetic, and united world by embracing this connection.

In honoring Dr. Wayne Dyer's legacy, I encourage you to embrace the Law of Divine Oneness in your own life. Recognize that you are not separate from those around you but rather an integral part of a greater whole. Approach your relationships, your work, and your life with a sense of unity and interconnectedness. Let compassion and empathy guide your actions, and let understanding our shared existence inspire you to lead with love and kindness.

As mentors, leaders, and individuals, we can create ripples of positive change that extend far beyond our immediate circles. By living in alignment with the Law of Divine Oneness, you can build a world where unity, compassion, and love are the driving forces behind everything we do. This is the legacy I strive to leave—a legacy that honors the teachings of Dr. Wayne Dyer and the many mentors who have shaped my journey.

In the words of Dr. Wayne Dyer, "Do not die with the music still inside you." Let this remind us that giving perpetually and shifting our perspectives to one of divine oneness can change our lives and the world around us.

JON KOVACH JR.

About Jon Kovach Jr.: Jon is an award-winning international motivational speaker and global mastermind leader. Jon has helped multi-billion-dollar corporations exceed their annual sales goals, including Coldwell Banker Commercial, Outdoor Retailer Cotopaxi, and the Public Relations Student Society of America. In addition, in his work as an accountability coach and mastermind facilitator, Jon has helped thousands of professionals overcome their challenges and achieve their goals by implementing his accountability strategies and Irrefutable Laws of High Performance. Jon is the Founder and Chairman of Champion Circle, a networking association that combines high-performance-based networking activities and recreational fun to create connection capital and increase prosperity for professionals. Jon is the Mastermind Facilitator and Team Lead of the Habitude Warrior Mastermind and the Global Speakers Mastermind & Masterclass founded by Speaker Erik "Mr. Awesome" Swanson.

Jon speaks on accountability, The Irrefutable Laws of High Performance, and The Power of Mastermind Methodologies. He is a #1 Bestselling Author and a featured keynote on SpeakUp TV, an Amazon Prime TV series, with his keynote speech titled, *Getting Unstuck*. In addition, he stars in over 100 speaking stages, podcasts, and live international summits each year. Jon's motivational messages have been viewed by over 300,000 people online. His voice has been used by global brands and creators on TikTok and Instagram Reels, such as: Red Bull USA, Michael Bublé, The NHL, Powell Books, GoDaddy Studio, Canada's Wonderland Amusement Park, and the LSU Cheer Team.

Author's website: *www.SpeakerJonKovachJr.com*

Book Series Website: *www.TheBookOfMentors.com*

HONORING DR. WAYNE DYER

JULIE DELGADILLO

SELF MENTORSHIP & RECIPROCAL EMPOWERMENT

. . . .

Mentorship has always been an anchor of mine. More than just guidance, mentoring is an experience that transforms both mentor and mentee in equal measure. In previous chapters in this series, I've shared how mentoring has guided my life—from the early days when I learned leadership through my parents' influence to pivotal moments when mentors such as Miss Hazel and Barbara helped me realize my potential.

What happens, then, once one has received mentorship and all that wisdom and support? How do we apply it in life and pass it along? Now, I find myself at an impasse where mentorship becomes something I embody rather than something to seek.

Mentorship as a Mutual Relationship

I have realized that mentorship is not a linear path—instead, it is more cyclical; giving and receiving are interwoven in their existence. Mentors have played an instrumental role in shaping my path while learning something valuable from me. Mentorship's powerful legacy lies within this reciprocity: its essence rests within its ability to recognize that, although people seek guidance, they also bring something of their own to offer in return.

Unknowingly, I found myself serving as an unwitting mentor. It happened unexpectedly during one of those everyday interactions you

169

might take for granted: A young woman in my community approached me asking for advice on balancing work and personal life. She admired my work while telling me she admired me as someone who had it all together despite her struggles. This realization was full circle for me when I realized that those challenges I had overcome could serve as roadmaps to others needing advice and mentorship.

Mentorship isn't about having all the answers; instead, it is about sharing our journey, lessons, and vulnerabilities—walking alongside someone while they navigate their path with support when necessary, offering assistance when they stumble, or celebrating their victories as though they were your own! I was lucky to become friends with this young lady as she and I became mentor-mentee relationships—her unique perspective inspired me to keep pushing through even when the going got tough!

Mentorship is an evolving concept. My consideration of my mentors has allowed me to witness an evolution in how I view and approach mentorship. At first, mentors provided resources, and knowledge gaps were filled by providing tools like Miss Hazel (described in previous chapter contributions). She helped me navigate academic challenges while instilling confidence and resilience, which served me through an extremely transformative period by showing my potential and aligning me with my purpose.

Now, I find myself at another stage of mentorship, one where the boundaries between mentor and mentee blur more fluidly than ever. Mentorship doesn't just involve learning from more experienced people; rather, it should include taking advantage of all possible sources of wisdom if we allow it. Everyone you come into contact with has something valuable to impart if only we listen.

Mentorship is a collaborative experience. I no longer view it as something for which I need an external instructor as much as something I seek internally through peers and colleagues, including friends, mentees, or anyone who may seem unrelated. Some of my most influential mentors may even remain unaware that they're mentoring me; friends, colleagues or even my mentees provide challenges, push my comfort zone away and illuminate parts of myself that I may have otherwise failed to recognize fully.

Mentorship as an Agent of Change

Empowerment has always been at the core of my work, and mentorship plays a central role. Mentorship doesn't provide new power but reveals their existing power for greater independence. I strive to foster strengths by nurturing them to help discover potential within them while offering the support necessary to navigate any potential roadblocks they might come up against in life.

One of the greatest joys of mentoring others is witnessing their transformations. I have had the honor of mentoring many women and young people over time, and the greatest moments have come when they begin seeing themselves as I see them: capable, strong, and full of potential. Mentorship should not involve forcing someone into being someone they aren't; rather, it should assist individuals in becoming their very best selves.

Maria came to me feeling uncertain about herself and her career path yet lacking the confidence to step into them powerfully. Through our conversations and the challenges I offered her, over time, Maria began seeing herself differently, taking risks more frequently, speaking up more, and taking up opportunities she previously avoided. Watching Maria transform into an empowered leader is truly one of my life's most satisfying experiences!

Maria's journey taught me an invaluable lesson about patience in mentorship. Personal and professional growth does not occur overnight; it requires hard work, dedication, encouragement, and persistence from everyone involved. Mentors must remain patient while giving our mentees the space they need to develop, remembering that our role as supporters should not include pushing.

Self-Mentorship is Essential

As much as I appreciate having mentors, one of the greatest sources of guidance and strength can come from within yourself. Self-mentorship involves applying lessons you've learned from others into your everyday life while becoming your biggest cheerleader, guide, and source of strength.

As I matured, I became less dependent on external mentors to guide me. Now that I trust myself more and listen to myself more closely, I seek guidance within myself more frequently rather than externally. That doesn't mean I no longer seek mentorship from others—quite the opposite, in fact—but rather that I know how to balance external guidance with internal wisdom.

Reflection has become one of my primary forms of self-mentorship, helping to keep me grounded and focused even when the road ahead may not always seem clear. I take time every week to reflect upon past experiences, examine lessons learned, and decide how they might apply in my everyday life moving forward. This practice has proven essential in staying grounded and focused no matter the obstacles.

Self-compassion is another critical aspect of self-mentorship that I found indispensable. Recognizing your humanity and realizing you will make mistakes is essential to treating yourself with the kindness and understanding you would show a mentee. Self-compassion has proven invaluable in helping me face life's obstacles with grace and resilience.

Mentorship isn't something to graduate from—it evolves with your life stages. My focus as a mentor lies in supporting others to become mentors while continuing my growth by finding opportunities to learn from others, challenge assumptions, and expand my understanding of what it means to mentor someone else. Successful mentors remain open-minded to new experiences while continually expanding on what they have discovered as mentors.

Accepting Mentorship as a Compass of Success

Technology has unleashed unimagined possibilities for connection and learning, making it simpler than ever to locate mentors worldwide. Virtual mentorship programs, online communities, and digital resources have revolutionized how mentors are approached, opening up endless doors of potential growth for both the mentor and mentee.

So, while we embrace new tools and technologies for mentorship, it's still vitally important to remember its core essence—relationships, connection, a shared journey of growth and empowerment. Trust, respect, and mutual learning still hold true whether mentoring someone offline or online.

Digital mentorship can be just as impactful in my work. Throughout my mentoring experiences with women and young people from diverse cultures spanning multiple countries through video calls, emails, and online platforms, my engagement has expanded my perspective while deepening my appreciation of global challenges and opportunities.

As time progresses, I remain committed to exploring innovative methods of mentoring and being mentored in today's digital environment. By harnessing technology as we do so, mentorship can reach further—creating a more connected and empowered society in its wake.

Steps for Becoming an Effective Mentor

Are you starting your mentorship journey? Below, I offer some practical steps I took to become an effective mentor. These may change with time as you gain experience, but nonetheless, they provide a solid framework upon which meaningful mentoring relationships may form.

1. **Active Listening:** One essential skill any mentor must master is active listening. Active listening goes beyond simply hearing what your mentee says—it involves understanding their needs, concerns, and aspirations without passing judgment. It gives each member of your mentee's community the space and respect they deserve to voice their opinions freely and independently. Take the time to actively

listen without judgment so your mentee knows their voice has been heard!

2. **Ask Thought-Provoking Questions:** A mentor's primary job is not to supply all the answers for their mentee but instead help them discover them themselves. Asking thoughtful questions that encourage introspection and critical thought processes among your mentees helps your mentor delve more deeply into their thoughts and emotions while stimulating critical thought for future decisions made by their mentees.

3. **Share Your Experiences:** Be bold and open up about your journey's successes and failures with your mentee; being vulnerable with them can build trust and rapport between both of you.

4. **Provide Constructive Feedback:** Feedback is critical for growth but must be delivered properly in order to be most beneficial. Focus on providing constructive comments that highlight improvement areas while acknowledging and celebrating strengths within their mentee's person.

5. **Encourage Self-Reflection:** Encourage your mentee to use reflection as an effective method for personal growth and increasing self-awareness. When used properly, reflection can provide immense potential benefits and deepen self-knowledge.

6. **Celebrate Their Achievements:** Acknowledging and celebrating your mentee's victories is crucial in building their confidence and reinforcing positive behaviors. Acknowledging achievements helps reinforce positive behaviors while building self-confidence.

7. **Be Patient & Supportive:** Growth takes time, so when setbacks arise, mentors and mentees should remain supportive and remind themselves that setbacks are an inevitable part of the learning process.

8. **Foster Independence:** Mentorship should provide your mentees with the confidence and tools they need to become independent, self-

sufficient individuals. Please encourage them to make decisions based on themselves alone while having faith in themselves and trusting in themselves and their capabilities.

Mentorship creates an ever-widening circle. When you mentor someone, you not only directly impact their life, but your influence also grows throughout their circle of influence. This effect creates lasting change while building communities of empowered individuals working toward a positive impact in our world.

One of the greatest joys of mentoring lies in seeing your mentees carry forward the lessons and values you've imparted. You see them mentor others with passion and dedication similar to what was shown to them. You know that your impactful mentorship will last beyond you, leaving an everlasting legacy of empowerment spanning generations.

As part of my work with Corazon and my personal life, I have witnessed firsthand the ripple effect mentorship has on the lives around me. One act can spark another and transform multiple lives through mentoring alone —this is truly amazing and represents its true power: making an impactful impression across communities that you may never fully comprehend!

Mentorship is one of the greatest gifts anyone can give; all it requires to be effective as a mentor is listening, sharing knowledge, and assisting on others' journey.

Mentorship can be an incredible catalyst for change—for mentors and mentees alike. Please take full advantage of its potential, share your light, and continue the journey, knowing its legacy will linger long into the future.

JULIE DELGADILLO

About Julie Delgadillo: Julie Delgadillo is a confident, enthusiastic, witty, and sought-after passionate servant leader and mentor with over 20 years of experience in non-profit management, leadership development, and confidence coaching. Julie is the Executive Director of Corazón U.S. & Mexico. Julie is a firm believer in leading by example and actively engages in developing community leaders. It's not uncommon to catch her rolling up her sleeves and wearing a toolbelt to personally contribute to building homes in Mexico for deserving low-income families.

Julie's strengths and passions are rooted in empowering women to be confidence in every area of their lives. Julie has personally coached and developed teens and women from across the globe and serves as an International Ambassador for the economic development of women. Julie is also a former International Beauty Queen and a long-time Hunger Relief Advocate.

An alumna of the prestigious University of Notre Dame's Mendoza School of Business Non-Profit Business Management Executive Leadership Program, Julie's educational journey is a testament to her commitment to growth and learning. Her undergraduate studies at Mount Saint Mary College and her certification in transformational life coaching from the Life Purpose Institute further enrich her holistic approach to empowerment. When she is not out conquering the world, you can find her discovering new brunch spots, listening to audiobooks, or in the aisles of TJ Maxx, Marshall's, or HomeGoods. Let's Connect: *www.Linkedin.com/in/JulieDelgadillo*

Author's Website: *www.linktr.ee/SheConquersTheWorld*

Book Series Website: *www.TheBookOfMentors.com*

KELLI HUDSON-KEY

MENTORSHIP IN A CHANGING WORLD

Mentorship has always been a cornerstone of my personal and professional life. Over the years, I've had the privilege of mentoring others and being mentored by some of the most brilliant minds in the business and the direct sales industry.

As I reflect, the theme that emerges most powerfully is the delicate balance between fear and faith (which is a continuation of the discourses on mentorship, expanding on the lessons learned and the wisdom I wrote in the first two books of this series.). Mentorship isn't just about passing on skills or knowledge; it's about guiding someone through their fears and the unknown with faith that the journey will be worth it. One of my favorite quotes is from Zig Ziglar. "FEAR can have two meanings, 'Forget Everything and Run ' or 'Face Everything and Rise.' The choice is yours."

Mentorship is not confined to the exchange of professional expertise; it is an intricate dance between guiding and learning, stepping out in faith, and managing fear. Over the years, I've learned that mentorship often means leading others out of their comfort zones and into the spaces where they can grow the most. This requires courage—not just on the mentee's part but also on the mentor's part. Wayne Dyer often said, "You cannot always control what goes on outside. But you can   control what goes on inside."

However, as time goes on, I've noticed that the dynamics of mentorship have begun to shift, especially in the aftermath of global events like the COVID-19 pandemic in 2020.

Generational Mentorship & the New Normal

When I think about mentorship, it reminds me of the importance of generational wisdom. I've always believed in the power of passing down knowledge from one generation to the next. This concept has shaped my approach to leadership and personal development. However, recent years have introduced new challenges that have changed how we connect, share, and grow.

COVID-19, for instance, has altered the landscape of mentorship in ways we never anticipated. People have become more isolated and, in many cases, more introverted. The need to peel back the layers of our emotions, fears, and insecurities has become even more crucial. We've all seen it: people who were once outgoing and social are now hesitant to engage, preferring the safety of their own space. This shift has made mentorship more complex, requiring deeper connections and more meaningful interactions.

One of the biggest challenges I've faced as a mentor is convincing people of the importance of regular, face-to-face communication—even if it's virtual. There's something incredibly powerful about hearing a voice, seeing a face, and feeling that connection, even through a screen. Yet, in a world where everyone prefers text messages and emails, maintaining that personal touch has become increasingly difficult.

Also, it's important to note that mentorship doesn't end with the mentor and the mentee; it's a legacy that continues through generations. I've had the privilege of mentoring many women throughout my career, and one of the most rewarding aspects of this journey has been seeing how the lessons I've shared have been passed down to others.

My daughter, for example, recently left her well-paying job in film production to start her own company with her husband. Watching her step out in faith, even when it was scary, reminded me of my journey.

She could have stayed in her comfortable position, but she chose to follow her passion and create something of her own.

I've observed this generational mentorship in many women I've worked with. They take the lessons they've learned and pass them on to their children, their colleagues, and their communities. It's a domino effect that starts with one person and extends far beyond what we can see.

The key to this kind of mentorship is teaching others what to do and showing them how to listen to their inner voice and trust their intuition. It's about helping them develop the courage to take risks and the faith to believe that those risks will lead to something greater. If done carefully, with the knowledge and approach of caring, deeper connection, and allowing faith over fear to thrive, I believe many will accept and respond positively to a higher level of mentorship—the new normal.

"You don't have to be great to start, but you have to start to be great."
~ Zig Ziglar

The Layers of Mentorship: From Surface to Substance

Previously, mentorship often focused on surface-level goals: improving skills, gaining knowledge, and achieving specific outcomes. But today, mentorship requires much more. It's about peeling back the layers of a person's identity, understanding their fears, dreams, and vulnerabilities, and creating a safe space to confront their weaknesses and turn them into strengths.

I've always emphasized that a good mentor isn't just someone who cheers you on from the sidelines. A good mentor isn't afraid to point out your weaknesses—not as a form of criticism, but as an opportunity for growth. This is why I believe mentorship needs to be separate from family relationships. Family members, self-proclaimed success coaches, and accountability partners who lack experience and evidence of past success may not always be objective in pointing out where you need to improve. However, a mentor can see the areas where you're struggling and help you navigate them with honesty and compassion. One of my favorite quotes is from an unlikely source, former NFL Coach, Tom

Landry. He said, "A coach is someone who tells you what you don't want to hear, who has you see what you don't want to see, so you can be who you have always known you could be."

Mentorship Beyond the Professional: Life Lessons Passed Down

Mentorship is not just about career advancement; it's about life. It's about teaching others how to serve, be grateful, and pass on the lessons they've learned to the next generation.

One of the most important lessons I've passed on to my children is the value of service. We live in a world that often prioritizes self-interest over the well-being of others, but true success comes from serving others. I've not only taught my children this but have also emphasized it to those I mentor.

Another critical lesson is the importance of gratitude. It's easy to get caught up in pursuing success and forget to be thankful for what you already have. But I've found that the more grateful you are, the more success you attract. Gratitude is a magnet for blessings, and I encourage everyone to cultivate it daily. There are five health benefits of practicing gratitude daily:

1. Improved overall physical health.

2. Improved overall psychological health.

3. Better quality sleep.

4. Better relationships.

5. Improved desire to give back.

I believe in the 4 A's of gratitude: appreciation, approval, admiration, and attention. By incorporating these four elements into your life, you'll boost your own self-esteem and that of others.

Also, I've learned that teaching others what you've learned is the best way to succeed. This is the essence of mentorship. It's about passing on your knowledge, experiences, and wisdom to the next generation so they can build on what you've started.

The Role of Confidence, Action, & Schedule in Achieving Goals

Throughout my career, I've seen countless people struggle to achieve their goals, not because they lack the skills or knowledge but because they lack three key elements: a solid schedule, consistent action, and confidence. These are the pillars of success and often the areas where I see the most resistance.

Let's talk about schedules. A mentor's role often involves helping someone create and stick to a schedule. It sounds simple, but it's one of the most challenging aspects of personal development. Life gets busy, distractions arise, and your goals have taken a back seat before you know it. As a mentor, work with mentees to develop a schedule that aligns with their goals and accommodates life's unpredictability.

But having a schedule is just the first step. The second—and equally important—step is taking action. It's one thing to know what you need to do; it's another to do it. This is where confidence comes into play. I've found that many people don't follow through with their plans simply because they lack the confidence to do so. They second-guess themselves, hesitate, and ultimately miss out on opportunities.

The Power of Self-Starting: A Discipline of Daily Habits

One of the most significant challenges I've seen in those I mentor, especially in entrepreneurship, is the struggle to self-start. Working for yourself is a different ball game than working for a boss. It requires a level of discipline that many people need to prepare for, and it's one of the key reasons why some succeed while others don't.

The first step in being a successful self-starter is understanding your "why." Why do you want to run your own business? Why do you want to take on this challenge? If your passion isn't bigger than your problems, you won't have the motivation to push through when things get tough.

I often ask people to dig deep and think about what drives them. Most of the time, the answer isn't money. It's a desire for freedom, flexibility, and the sense of accomplishment that comes from building something of your own. It's about wanting something you can point to and say, "I did this."

Once you've identified your why, the next step is to create and stick to a plan. Success is found in your daily habits. It's about showing up daily, even when you don't like it. It's about doing the hard things first—those tasks that intimidate you or make you uncomfortable—because those are the things that will move you forward.

I teach people to break down their goals into manageable steps, sometimes as small as 15 minutes of focused work at a time. This can be the difference between success and failure for those just starting. It's not about working for hours on end; it's about being consistent and disciplined in the time that you do have. These steps can create greater faith, confidence, and competence in anyone's career. Tom Landy said, "The secret to winning is constant, consistent management."

Mentorship in a Post-Pandemic World

The world has changed, and so has the way we mentor. A new layer of complexity has been added to the mentor-mentee relationship. People are more guarded, introverted, and hesitant to open up. As a mentor, it's my job to break through those barriers, peel back the layers, and help my mentees reach their full potential.

In response to these changes, I've had to adapt my approach to mentorship. I've learned to be more patient, more empathetic, and more understanding of each person's unique challenges. I've also had to become more creative in connecting with my mentees, using technology to bridge the gap and create meaningful interactions.

For example, upon arriving home from a work-sponsored vacation, it was immediately thrust upon us that we had to take everything we had built, including an in-person face-to-face business meeting model, and completely uproot that way of thinking and conduct business through a virtual platform like Zoom. Although it seemed like my world and entire career had just been flipped upside down overnight, we all had to adapt rapidly to get ahead of the worldwide changes. I felt like I became a "How to Use Zoom for Face-to-Face Sales Meetings" consultant overnight—not bad for someone who had never used nor had to use Zoom their entire life before this event.

If there's one thing I want to leave with those who read this chapter, it's the importance of not waiting. Don't wait to pursue your dreams. Don't wait to take that leap of faith. Life is short, and you don't know how much time you have to make an impact.

One of the greatest gifts we can give to those we mentor is the courage to step into the unknown. I've had to do this many times, and it's always been worth it.

The Difference Between Help & Support

One of the critical distinctions I've made over the years is the difference between helping and supporting someone. Help implies doing something for someone that they can't do themselves. Support, on the other hand, is about guiding someone as they do the work themselves. As a mentor, I'm not here to solve your problems for you. I'm here to support you through them, offering guidance, wisdom, and encouragement.

This distinction is crucial because it empowers the mentee to take ownership of their journey. When you support someone rather than help them, you give them the tools they need to succeed independently. You're teaching them how to fish rather than just giving them a fish. This approach not only builds confidence but also fosters independence and resilience. "A lot of people have gone further than they thought they could because someone else thought they could," said Zig Ziglar

The Essentials of Success: Unchanged, Yet Evolving

Despite the changes in how we mentor, the core values and characteristics that lead to success remain unchanged. Hard work, dedication, integrity, and perseverance are the foundation for success. What has changed is the way we instill these values in others. The dynamics of mentorship have shifted, but the goal remains the same: to help others achieve their full potential.

Mentorship today requires more than imparting knowledge. It requires a deep understanding of the human experience, a willingness to connect personally, and the ability to adapt to a rapidly changing world. It's about seeing the whole person—their strengths, weaknesses, and potential—and guiding them to become their best version.

The Future of Mentorship

As I look to the future, I'm excited about the possibilities of mentorship in this new era. Yes, there are challenges, but there are also incredible opportunities to make a lasting impact on the lives of others. By embracing these changes and continuing to evolve our approach, we can ensure that mentorship remains a powerful tool for personal and professional growth.

The world may be different, but the need for mentorship is stronger than ever. And as long as people are willing to learn, grow, and achieve their dreams, I'll be here—ready to support them every step of the way.

KELLI HUDSON-KEY

About Kelli Hudson-Key: Kelli Hudson-Key has built a remarkable career that speaks volumes of her dedication, leadership, and passion. Currently, she holds the esteemed position of Senior Division Executive at Park Lane Jewelry. In this role, she plays an instrumental part in the company's growth and success, leading her team with a unique blend of wisdom and enthusiasm.

Before her tenure at Park Lane Jewelry, Kelli showcased her prowess in the realm of direct sales with Mary Kay Inc., a global powerhouse known for its impressive legacy spanning 60 years in the beauty industry. For over 22 years, she contributed significantly to the brand as Senior Sales Director. During this time, Kelli was integral in fostering the company's sales strategies, solidifying its position as one of the leading direct sellers of personal beauty products in the United States.

Her longevity and success in the industry is a testament to Kelli's unparalleled drive and commitment. Her knack for understanding market dynamics, combined with her talent for nurturing and guiding her teams, has marked her as a leading figure in the direct sales sector. In every endeavor, Kelli Hudson-Key's name is synonymous with excellence, leadership, and an unwavering commitment to success around the world.

Message me at: *m.me/Kelli.HudsonKey*

Author's Website: *www.MyParkLane.com/KelliKey*

Book Series Website: *www.TheBookOfMentors.com*

LAUREN COBB

MENTORSHIP OF THE MIND

"Peace is the result of retraining your mind to process life as it is, rather than as you think it should be."
~ **Dr. Wayne Dyer**

I love this quote from Dr. Wayne Dyer.

I have learned this over the years, and it's served me well. Retraining my thought process has allowed me to live a fuller life.

When I was nineteen, my Dad passed away from kidney cancer. From diagnosis to when he passed was nine months. Those nine months were the longest months of my life. My family and I were left in a position where everyone around us didn't know how to act. Dad was very well-known and respected, and I loved that about him. He was an example of loving and serving those he interacted with.

However, it became SO hard to go anywhere. I mourned and had many hard days and nights of sorrow and when I left the house it seemed to follow me. If I seemed okay, people would then ask me how my mom was, and how my siblings were doing and would assume we were all just sad. It got to a point where I was ready to move—I wanted to move and have a fresh start where people got to know me for me and not my past.

One Sunday, I went to church in a new congregation and what a relief it was that I was able to sit through a whole meeting and not be patted on the back with condolences or have someone shrug as they approached me asking how everyone was holding up. It was a much-needed change.

I could go to the grocery store and not see someone who knows my family and so on. I felt like I was finally able to become myself and a married couple with my new husband. Now, it wasn't that I was shoving my grieving aside—I definitely went through the many stages of grief— but once I was away from the constant sadness that people had when they talked with me, I was able to find a more positive outlook.

It surely sucked to lose my Dad so young. At eighteen, I was caring for my Dad full-time. That's not what most eighteen-year-olds are doing. Those thoughts would creep in on how unfair I was in that situation. I didn't have a Daddy-Daughter Dance at my wedding; I don't have pictures of my Dad holding my babies in the hospital. Thankfully, by the time I had babies, I was in the part of life where I had accepted life as it is. I had strong convictions that my Dad was there with my babies as they came to earth. He held them up in heaven until they got to come to us here on earth.

I've been able to recognize blessings in my life that came because of the hard things I went through. I was able to spend precious time with my grandparents as they were in the last stages of their earthly life, and I knew how to care for them. Things that always scared me growing up are now just another part of life. It doesn't mean I enjoy the hard parts, but I can see the silver lining and know I can still be happy.

I have learned that life isn't just happening to me—I get to experience life and create the life I want and pivot as needed. I feel such peace when I repeat that sentence above.

I truly believe that when we don't give into self-pity and doubt, more abundance and opportunities find us.

A metaphor Dr. Wayne Dyer shared goes, "When you squeeze an orange, orange juice comes out, because that's what's inside. When you are squeezed, what comes out is what is inside us."

What do we do to ensure what is inside of us will help us when we're being squeezed?

1. Surround yourself with others whose insides are filled with greatness! They say the five people you spend the most time with are a reflection of yourself. Make them good ones!

2. Fill your mind and heart with gratitude.

3. Strive daily to read uplifting messages and books... Books like this.

4. Be sure you're applying the things you're learning every day!

5. Keep a journal of the hard times and the good times. How did you respond compared to how you felt on the inside? You want those to align. You can only keep a happy face for so long.

6. If needed, seek out help from professionals.

7. Serve those around you. Serving people grows and can turn surface-level relationships into trusted relationships, then lead to perpetual relationships—the kind where you know they've got your back, and they know you've got theirs.

8. Every month or so, self-reflect. Are you being true to yourself and your beliefs? Are you in alignment with your desires? If not, pivot and find the people and resources to get you on the right track.

Doing these things will help you grow and become the person you want to become at a much faster pace. You will become one of those people who doesn't let life dictate their decisions and feelings. You take the reins and direct your life where you want to go!

Here is a brief list of things that I do daily to ensure I'm on the path I want to be on.

- Daily prayer.

- Meditation and envisioning my life as I want it to play out.

- Learn—I dive into books and podcasts that uplift me and or teach me new things.

- I take care of my physical body, whether that's a good workout or walking or giving my body much-needed rest. This also includes what I feed my body, being aware of how foods make me feel and how my body performs.
- Setting boundaries with others.
- Starting new every day!

I love Dr. Wayne Dyer's way of explaining things—no beating around the bush, just straightforward, in a language you can understand and that feels easy to start applying.

Learning from the greats is one of my favorite things. They share from a place of wisdom and experience that we get to learn and apply in our lives, and doing so will not only set you aside from others but put you further ahead on the path to success.

LAUREN COBB

About Lauren Cobb: Lauren Cobb is a wife to her amazing and supportive husband Tyler. A mother to 3 beautiful daughters who've taught her more in the last 12 years than she has learned in the first 23 years of her life.

At a young age, Lauren knew she had a lot of ambition and drive. As she became an adult, she knew that entrepreneurship was her passion, and thankfully, she married someone who supported that! Together with Ty, they own a graphic and media design company that they've built from the ground up. Growing and seeing the successes of their own efforts has been one of the most rewarding experiences!

Self-development and leadership have been a big part of Lauren's life since she was 14. She traveled and taught leadership to youth across the country throughout her high school years. She knows first-hand how self-development is crucial to success in life. Knowing who you are and finding your purpose and passion is important.

As Lauren and her husband Ty are building their businesses and seeking a network and friends who are aligned with their values, they've found in Champion Circle and learned how to properly mastermind. Lauren is a member of the corporate executive team at Champion Circle Networking Association, founded and led by Jon Kovach Jr. Masterminds have changed her life and their business for the better.

Author's Website: *www.TyCobb.MyPortfolio.com*

Book Series Website: *www.TheBookOfMentors.com*

> *"EVERYTHING YOU ARE AGAINST WEAKENS YOU. EVERYTHING YOU ARE FOR EMPOWERS YOU."*
>
> ~ DR. WAYNE DYER

HONORING DR. WAYNE DYER

LIZ SEARS

BEWARE OF THE FALSE DICHOTOMY

"You just don't understand, Liz! I. Can't. Do. That!!!!!" he yells at me from the doorway.

"Ahhhh! If you fight for your limiting beliefs, you will ALWAYS have them!" I yell at him as he slams the door and walks away.

I sit on our bed, frustrated, furious, and despondent. We've been married for nearly 15 years, and I want him to see that he can be and do so much more than he is! When I look at him, I see someone with the most spectacular way to connect with practically anyone. I see a brilliant Activator, someone who can get others on board with his ridiculous ideas. I've seen him convince his family and friends to help him complete projects, and they have a blast while doing it. And I love how he lights up a room when he walks in because he's so fun!

Our argument started when I told him he could be so much more successful if he wanted to be. He had told me that he couldn't.

As I sit on our bed, I feel like a hypocrite. Sure, he could be more successful, but so could I! It's 2010, and our nation is in the middle of the Great Recession. My husband and I are both in real estate, and when the housing market crashed in 2008, our incomes dropped practically overnight. For two years, we've been desperately looking for how to shift our circumstances, and we often find ourselves in these fights. I'm tired. I'm overwhelmed. This is so hard.

Sometime later, I'm at my friend Nichole's house, and I see a book on her end table titled "Change Your Thoughts, Change Your Life" by Wayne Dyer. I pick it up and flip through a few pages, reading random passages, and as I read, I get goosebumps first on my arms, then up my scalp, and then down my legs. How have I never heard of Wayne Dyer before?? I've been a student of motivational writers and speakers for years, yet I'd never heard of him. Okay, this is changing—right now!

I open my Audible app and buy the first Wayne Dyer book that pops up. It's "How to Be a No-Limit Person." As soon as I leave Nichole's house, I start listening to it in my car. Surprisingly, it's not a book he wrote that he's reading; this is a compilation of his lectures. It's so good! A few hours later, I finish it and start it again. Over the years I've realized that if I listen to an audible book two times in a row, I remember so much more of what is taught. It's always fascinating to realize that these books are a lifetime of someone's learning distilled down into a single book.

I hear Wayne say, "Relax, let go, allow, and recognize that some of your desires are about how you think your world should be, rather than how it is in that moment. Become an astute observer." Then he says, "...judge less and listen more. Take time to open your mind to the fascinating mystery and uncertainty that we all experience."

Goosebumps again. I pause the book.

This is a turning point in my life. I can feel it.

So much of what I'm feeling frustrated about is my desire for how things "should" be instead of how they are. That old cliché runs through my mind, "the way to have everything in life is to believe you already do." For my entire life, I believed that if someone were truly content with what they had, they wouldn't need to strive for more. I also believed that if someone was setting goals, that meant they wanted something different than what they had, which also meant that they were discontent.

How does this all fit? "Relax, let go, allow...judge less and listen more." Okay. This is definitely applicable to the fight I just had. "...open your mind to the fascinating mystery."

"...the fascinating mystery."

"...open your mind..."

Then I saw it. I saw the false dichotomy!

It's not either or. It's not what I have now versus what I want. It's not contentment with my current situation versus striving for my goals. We are not meant to be stagnant, *and* we are not meant to be discontent. And that is the false dichotomy. It's recognizing that I can experience total contentment while also designing, striving for, and being excited about a brighter and bigger future. It's both, at the same time, working together to create an amazing life.

The path to do this is to "… judge less and listen more."

I realize that I constantly judge where I am at. I read all these motivational books, get inspired, and then use what they were trying to teach me to judge myself as lacking. All I see is where I "should" be, how I "should" show up or behave, how my house "should" be organized, or whatever I am currently reading. While this approach does help me grow as a person, it also leaves me feeling discontent and shame.

And I get goosebumps again but they're different. I realize I'm using the same approach to judge my husband and it's not working. All that this approach is doing is creating discontentment and shame for him, and bitterness and judgment from me. Yikes!

So, if the path is to "judge less," and since I already know that the opposite of judgment is gratitude, then gratitude is the bridge between our current state and achieving our goals.

It's choosing gratitude for what is happening right now. It's choosing to feel gratitude for where I'm at, for where my husband is at, for what's in our life, for the relationships we have, for the lessons we're learning, for where we'll be when we hit our goals, for everything. Sometimes horrible things happen, and in those moments, I can take time, if I need, to feel negative emotions. And when I'm ready, I can feel gratitude for the parts of my life that are not part of the horrible thing that happened.

This is a turning point in my life.

No longer will I read personal development books or self-evaluate to make myself wrong or to judge myself as lacking. Instead, I will view it as having an amazing personal coach! I will use what I read and any self-evaluation as personalized coaching. I'll use what resonates with me and leave the rest. I will take the coaching from an empowered, grateful perspective. I feel excited! I feel lighter. Did the room just get brighter?

This commitment to a new approach starts to improve everything. I'm shocked as I recognize how many times a day something isn't how it "should" be. I'm becoming an "astute observer," and it's a bit painful! My expectations of what "should" be and my frustrations when it's not have been making my life and my family's lives so much more miserable than they actually are! I'm learning how to communicate without making me wrong or them wrong. It's so new! It's much more peaceful.

And the best part is that now my husband's and my conversations about growth and goals are fun! We strive to use this completely new approach. It's more of a game now. Instead of thinking anything "should" be a certain way, we just figure out what we want next in our lives: better habits, better relationships, better health, more philanthropy, more adventure, more success, or anything else. Then we identify what we've got to work with (relationships, resources, skills...), and then we game plan how to use what we've got to get what we're striving for. We look back on that one fight so many years ago with gratitude for how we've learned this new way to approach creating a life we love.

LIZ SEARS

About Liz Sears: Liz Sears lives her life in every way to fulfill her life mission, which is to "inspire the masses to live lives full of connection, contribution, adventure, and impact." As a speaker and writer, she focuses on the consistency of striving toward becoming the best version of ourselves and sharing how to be awake and engaged in life. She fully believes that life, with its extensive variety of obstacles and opportunities, can be an amazing adventure. It's all about how we play the hand we were dealt and what we choose to create.

Liz has been married to her best friend since 1996, and together, they have raised four wonderful sons. She is a proud alumna of Kent-Meridian High School and pursued Business Administration/ Management at the University of Utah. Her roots trace back to Seattle, Washington, but she and her family now call Layton, Utah home.

Beginning in the financial industry in 1995, Liz's career path has included roles such as Mortgage Loan officer, Property Manager, Real Estate Investor, and most recently as Team Leader and Associate Broker of Utah's Elite | REALTORS® at Real Brokers, LLC. She has served many times in leadership roles in the Real Estate industry, including on the Board of Directors for the Northern Wasatch Association of Realtors and as a Governing Board Member of the Women's Council of Realtors Utah.

Author's Website: *www.UtahsEliteRealtors.com*

Book Series Website: *www.TheBookOfMentors.com*

M. A. FULTS

ANOTHER STONE FOR THE PATH

"When you dance, your purpose is not to get to a certain place on the floor. It's to enjoy each step along the way."
~ **Dr. Wayne Dyer**

In the last Book of Mentors, I proposed that each volume and chapter is its own Legacy Stone—a Stone along the path of whoever picks it up to read. A Stone that can be 'stepped' on multiple times. A Stone extending the Legacy of each honored mentor. Once again, it is an honor and a privilege to provide another stone to your pathway.

"Love is the ability and willingness to allow those that you care for to be what they choose for themselves without any insistence that they satisfy you."
~ Dr. Wayne Dyer

In *The Book of Mentors Volume 2, Honoring Bob Proctor*, I shared that the mentors through my lifetime have been numerous and varied. In that chapter, I provided many of the "Legacy Stones" I found in the books I'd read over six decades. In this chapter I will share the Stones I found in movies and television shows, essentially, in entertainment.

Some might question entertainment as being capable of 'mentoring,' yet, if I mention Steven Spielberg's "The Color Purple," what emotions does that evoke? What thoughts about redemption and resiliency do they bring to mind? How about the television series "Roots" or the movie "Beaches"? If those are not recent enough, what about "Schindler's List" or "A Beautiful Day In The Neighborhood"? Totally different movies and

201

themes, invoking different emotions and thoughts, but both are filled with life and truths, and, dare I add, heroics. All of these examples touched hearts and minds, making simple and complex statements on life, living, and living well. They provided examples both good and bad. And yes, they also entertained.

My earliest memory of watching a movie was "Mary Poppins" with Julie Andrews and Dick Van Dyke. My parents must have taken us to see it just before we traveled to Teheran, Iran, where my father was stationed at the U.S. Embassy. For me, this was between my first and second grades. Before we left for Iran, though, we were in Fort Leonard Wood, Missouri, and I can remember watching the small TV screen, around nine inches tall, with "Superman" and "Lassie" being my favorite shows.

Once in Teheran, though, TV watching was limited to one station, the Armed Forces Radio and Television Station (AFRTS). AFRTS had limited inventory, rotating the same shows and movies each year, and it only broadcasted eight-ten hours a day. Many of the programming limitations stemmed from the host country requiring specific shows not be broadcast where anyone—read: their citizens—could watch.

There were fairly recent movies played at the "Castle Club," an Air Force base Club with pool, baseball fields, tennis courts, an eating establishment, and a golf course. There is a joke there, often said in US Navy circles, but I'll refrain from USAF bashing. The Castle Club would host weekend bingo and movie nights during the summer months, but "Old Yeller" is the only movie I can remember. I do remember watching a movie on AFRTS, though. It was "Murder in the Rue Morgue," and it scared me out of the room the first time it came on. My older brother's teasing over the next few weeks didn't help. However, the next time it aired, a year later, I forced myself to watch to the end. Since I was at a friend's house, there was some peer pressure incentive, but the second time around, it wasn't as scary as the first viewing—lesson learned.

With only limited programming available, Dad found a way for us to watch many other shows. He arranged with the AFRTS personnel to bring home reels and a projector. This led to me being able to tease my older brother because included with the westerns and cop shows were documentaries—one of which was an autopsy.

Yes, I shake my head that my father allowed his two young children—I couldn't have been over nine years old, my bother maybe thirteen—to watch a full autopsy. But we did, or I did, as my brother ended up leaving the room (Dad bailed almost before it even started!). In all probability, a nine-year-old was too young to fully comprehend what she was watching, but the teasing was fun. A side benefit of this activity: We learned how to thread a projector, rewind reel to reels, and even to splice film.

"If you don't make peace with your past,
it will keep showing up in your present."
~ Dr. Wayne Dyer

Back in "The World," stateside, there were an amazing FOUR different channels to choose from, and shows were on almost all day long. But I don't remember many of them until we returned from the next overseas tour and I was exposed to "The Carol Burnett Show" for the very first time. Truthfully, that show had me on the floor laughing until my sides hurt, many, many times. The most memorable one, which still makes me laugh to this day, was their parody of "Gone With The Wind."

And though it was 'only' reruns, I was finally able to watch the original Star Trek. Carol helped me to develop a sense of humor, but Star Trek—wow, what a show. Today, the original may seem campy, but the themes dealt with in almost every episode were cutting-edge for the 1960s and still relevant today. One of the most memorable episodes guest-starred Frank Gorshin as a half-black-right side, half-white-left side man, with his enemy being the same half-black and half-white, just on opposite sides. And the first interracial kiss on television literally made history.

There were many memorable movies during the '70s and '80s, such as "The Way We Were," "M*A*S*H"—which had one of the best spin-off TV comedies-and "The Deer Hunter," all of which were remembered as impactful movies in their own way. However, my focus was on the movies from the 1940s and 1950s. Those old movies touched my heart and mind, from film noir to war-time pics, from books made into movies to episodic stories of love and struggle, wisdom and courage. My favorites include: "How Green Was My Valley," "Yankee Doodle Dandy," "They Were Expendable," "Dark Victory," and "Key Largo." I will still watch these films today. Many of the actors and actresses became my idols, leading to watching every movie made with James Cagney, Spenser Tracy, Katherine Hepburn, Betty Davis, Humphrey Bogart, John Wayne, and Lauren Bacall, to name just a few.

Each one brought something very special to the screen. Their characters inspired me, the stories moved and intrigued me, and the time spent in theatres ultimately drove me to want and pursue more and to be a better person, a better officer, a better leader. Whether hero or villain, lead or supporting, these actors and actresses helped me see worlds beyond my own limited environment. When I was young, I often heard I was too much of a dreamer, reaching too high for things that were, if not impossible, at best, a nice fantasy.

Yet, I did become an Officer in the US Navy, going to sea on multiple ships and even commanding my own. I took on positions and tasks for which I'd not studied or trained, but I knew I could do well with the assistance of those around me. But perhaps what those men and women, as well as child actors, taught me best was the importance of relationships because, in the end, what I remember best about my life is the people, the friendships, and the relationships found and kept.

I'll end this chapter the same way I did the last, emphasizing the importance of choosing mentors, or Legacy Stones, wisely. All of the movies and television shows listed above were good, as entertainment, but also in providing solid stones upon which I walked out my life. What isn't included is the number of shows I watched and left regretting the time spent. I have been known to leave a movie early or turn off a show before its end, though probably not as many as I should have. Thankfully, that list is not as long as it could be.

"Change your inner thoughts to the higher frequencies of love, harmony, kindness, peace, and joy, and you'll attract more of the same."
~ Dr. Wayne Dyer

In the end, everyone is encouraged to choose those things that bring you more love, joy, and peace. Those are the things to remember, as Legacy Stones, to walk on again and again, especially when you need more love, more joy, and more peace in your life.

M. A. FULTS

About M. A. (MaryAlice) Fults: Born into an Army family, and with 39 years serving in and then working for the US Navy, means Fults spent many years traveling and living in foreign countries including four years in Teheran, Iran. She has a BFA in Drama Production from the University of AZ and a MS in Management from Naval Postgraduate School in Monterey, CA. After retiring for the second time in 2022, Fults continued her life-long pursuit of learning, while embarking on her new found passion of Heart Healing, Financial Advising and Life-Coaching. She has been blessed with one son.

Book Series Website: *www.TheBookOfMentors.com*

MARIS SEGAL & KEN ASHBY

A GROUNDING LEGACY— QUOTES TO LIVE BY

Did you know that Wayne Dyer began his career as a guidance counselor? While we never had an opportunity to meet him, for decades, Dyer's work on the world stage of personal development has guided and shaped our lives as individuals and professionals from our teen era to now as a Couplepreneur, connected over twenty years in love and business.

Although no longer with us, Dyer's influence continues to offer pragmatic steppingstones that evolve and elevate our leadership at home, work, and in our community. From one level of our self-discovery to the next level of empowerment, so much of what Dyer gave us is reflected in the many celebrated quotes that are part of his grounding legacy. These are a few of our favorites that have supported our mindset, actions, and head-and-heart relational leadership work. As you explore these transformational quotes, perhaps for the first time, we invite you to truly experience them with a lens into your own life.

"When you judge another, you do not define them, you define yourself."
~ Dr. Wayne Dyer

Ken: Judgment often stems from the biases and beliefs we've absorbed from our upbringing and life experiences, which can trigger emotional reactions. This tendency of judgment creates a sense of disconnection in our relationships. Reflecting on this, I see the importance of respect.

When I was in high school, I would judge quickly without considering others' perspectives—not a great way to make lasting friendships. This close-minded judgment revealed my own limitations and harmed both my relationships and self-esteem. In those moments, it wasn't "them" who were lacking—it was "me!" How I reacted to them exposed my limiting beliefs, left them feeling bad and, at the same time, was not respecting myself!

My eyes and heart opened up in my teens when I was selected to travel the world as a student and singer-songwriter with the youth leadership arts organization, Up with People. I embarked on a global expedition of human curiosity and traveled and performed in over twenty countries. This experience greatly expanded with each new experience. I learned to see the world and all humans with a new perspective. Now, when a feeling of judgment comes up, I get curious about 1) Where is my reaction coming from? 2) What is the other person's perspective and why? 3) What will the consequences be of my actions? 4) Will I be able to face myself in the mirror and be proud of myself? Judgment and curiosity are a choice. Today, I endeavor to replace judgment with curiosity and watch the world evolve with greater respect!

> *"All blame is a waste of time."*
> ~ Dr. Wayne Dyer

We have one life to live, one body and one planet. Our relationships are the most significant factor impacting and influencing every aspect of our lives. Whether personally or professionally, we're in a relationship with someone or something from morning to night. We call this relationship immersion the RFactor! Relationships, like air, water, and time are constant and constantly changing. In our relationship with "time," unfolding in 24-hour cycles, the choices we make regarding time is everything. Like judgment, blame is also a choice. So, why choose to waste time with negativity, blaming others or ourselves when we can be so much more productive, life-giving, and joyful.

Wisdom teachers remind us that, when you point your finger at someone else, there are three more pointing back at you. Seriously, think about it: when you're busy deflecting and not being responsible, you're not actually fixing anything. Blaming someone else often means you're dodging responsibility. This Dyer quote also cracks open the idea of playing the "victim."

Here is a great example from a recent experience. During a recent band competition, a noticeable error occurred when a few off-key notes were played by the large horn section during one performance. The audience, consisting of family, friends, press, and community leaders, reacted with a brief collective gasp. It was evident that multiple players had made the mistake, but no specific individual could be identified by the audience. Each participant in the competition had practiced this segment, which had been confirmed during the final rehearsal the day before.

In the post-concert discussion, the conductor took responsibility for the mishap, citing the need for better communication and more practice on her part. Conversely, the band member leading the section attributed the error to not receiving a final decision about the change. Instead of admitting his lack of attendance at the last rehearsal and failure to read the final preparation email, he positioned himself as a victim of circumstances. These contrasting viewpoints highlight two distinct perspectives on the incident.

The amount of time it takes to navigate and get to the bottom of the blaming story becomes a time suck for all involved and is just not respectful or responsible. Instead of the blame game, the collective energy could be spent collaborating and actually addressing and solving the problem. Mistakes happen—owning them is so much easier than blame. Imagine our world if everyone stood responsibly in truth and chose to leave blame behind.

"You cannot be lonely if you like the person you're alone with."
~ Dr. Wayne Dyer

Maris: Who would you say your most important relationship is with? Arguably, even before family, friends or faith, your relationship with yourself is paramount. YOU are the one relationship you can't leave home without! This Dyer quote really hits home and sits as a cornerstone of our head and heart leadership coaching and consulting. Studies show that how you are feeling inside about yourself, your self-worth, and the messages and chatter (positive and/or negative) that you are saying to yourself directly impact how you show up all day with friends, family, and at work! It is an inside out job!

I'm the youngest of three girls and ten cousins in a close-knit Jewish family. While we lived in three different states, weekend and holiday gatherings at Grandma's were always a playful adventure! With an age gap ranging from 3-12 years, I often felt like I did not belong. One day, frustrated by not being included in a game they were all playing, I said to my grandmother (who I adored), that I was lonely and bored. Her immediate reply was, "Bored!? When you like yourself, you can always be entertained and never feel lonesome."

That's my earliest memory of learning to be with me! I remember thinking, "Heck, if I didn't want to spend time with me, why would anyone else!?" My value since childhood has come from my mission to support others, be sure they have a voice, and bring a smile to someone's face. That said, I was a perfectionist and had belonging and self-confidence issues that, even with my accomplishments, still plagued me into my adulthood.

In my youth, I recall my parents reminding us to "be kind to others" and "respect others" and what I learned early in my professional life that I know to be true is that kindness and respect begin inside. Only then can we be there for others. Gratitude is also another powerful tool in learning to like ourselves. Both Ken and I have confronted the moment in our lives when we got to understand how to genuinely enjoy our own company, be true to ourselves, and become the people we want to hang out with.

When I am kind to myself and stand in gratitude, recognizing my value and all the amazing possibilities around me, I'm comfortable in my own skin and at peace with who I am. From this space, being alone becomes less about solitude and more about self-discovery. We all have a constant companion in ourselves, someone who understands us like no one else can. So yes, if you can be cool with you, even though you may be alone, you don't have to be lonely. My grandmother asked me what I liked about myself. This is the question I pose to you. Have you met yourself lately?

Wayne Dyer's wisdom remains a poignant reminder that our perceptions of others are a reflection of our inner landscape rather than a true depiction of those we judge. His belief that blame is futile emphasizes the need to channel our energies into constructive solutions rather than fixating on assigning fault. As we navigate the intricacies of daily human interaction, the evolution of our relationships begins with introspection and self-awareness. This shift toward inner growth fosters healthier and more meaningful connections with others.

Thank you, Wayne W. Dyer!

MARIS SEGAL & KEN ASHBY

About Maris Segal & Ken Ashby: Ken Ashby and Maris Segal, "America's Master Connectors," coach, consult, and collaborate with executives, entrepreneurs, celebrities and rising leaders to identify and bring their professional, personal, and philanthropic vision to life. Spanning four decades and forty countries, they combine their relationship marketing expertise with head and heart leadership to build meaningful connections and impactful strategies that drive their client's internal and external success.

Ken and Maris live by the philosophy, "We are all connected as humans first, and that's where the bottom line begins."

Together and individually, working across the public and private sectors, they have served a wide spectrum of local and global leaders, consumer and financial brands, causes, and policymakers. This dynamic duo also leverages Ken's international award-winning singer-songwriting gifts to develop collaborative teams with a songwriting workshop series. From board rooms and classrooms to Harvard, the White House, and Super Bowl Halftimes, Ken and Maris are also known for uniting diverse populations with innovative cross-cultural marketing and personal development programs.

As certified Executive and Relationship coaches, their latest book, *The RFactor; Universal Rhythms for Leading Prosperous Relationships* and their **DRIVE method: D**esire, **R**elationships, **I**ntention, **V**ision, and **E**mpowerment sit at the core of their work. Ashby and Segal set a path for every client to build high performing businesses and elevate personal and professional leadership for maximum impact and a 360-degree thriving life! As authors they have been featured in thirteen Amazon Bestselling leadership centered books. They speak regularly and were recently featured on the TEDx Farmingdale stage.

Author's Website: *www.SegalLeadershipGlobal.com*

Book Series Website: *www.TheBookOfMentors.com*

MEL CARR

THE POWER OF INTENTION & PRESENCE IN BUSINESS

When I first came across Dr. Wayne Dyer's work, I didn't expect it to impact me as much as it did. To be honest, I don't buy into everything he talks about, but a couple of ideas stuck with me and have made a big difference in how I run my life and my businesses. Those ideas are the power of intention and the importance of being present.

Setting Intentions that Matter

One of the things Dr. Dyer often talked about was the power of intention —how what you focus on and put your energy into can shape your reality. This idea clicked with me because I've seen it play out in my own journey.

When I started Cloversy, I wasn't just thinking about building a business. I wanted to create something that made a difference, not just for me but for the people I work with and for our clients. I set the intention that Cloversy would be more than just another virtual assistant service—it would be a place where women could find meaningful work, where we could support each other, and where our clients would feel truly cared for.

That intention shaped every decision I made. It wasn't just about offering a service but building a community and a culture where everyone feels valued. And I believe that's why Cloversy has grown the way it has. It's not just about the work we do; it's about the energy and intention behind it.

The same goes for The Six-Figure Chicks. When I launched this project, I intended to create a space where women entrepreneurs could celebrate their successes and inspire others. I wanted it to be a community where we could lift each other and share our stories, not in a competitive way, but in a way that shows there's room for all of us to succeed. Setting that intention has helped shape what The Six-Figure Chicks has become—a supportive, empowering group of women who are all about lifting each other.

Intentions are powerful because they guide our actions, even in the small, everyday things. For example, when I'm writing content for our websites or planning social media posts, I'm not just thinking about what will get the most likes or shares. I'm thinking about how the content aligns with our core values and how it can genuinely help or inspire someone. This shift in focus—from just getting results to making an impact—has been a game-changer for both of my businesses.

And it's not just about big-picture intentions either. I try to apply this mindset in everything we do at Cloversy and The Six-Figure Chicks. Whether it's a simple email to a client, a team meeting, or planning our next big project, I ask myself, "What's the intention behind this? How does this align with the bigger picture?" This has helped me stay focused and grounded, even when things get hectic.

Being Present in the Moment

Another idea from Dr. Dyer that I've taken to heart is the importance of being present. Let's be honest—running a business (or two) can be chaotic. There's always something to do, and getting caught up in the whirlwind of tasks, goals, and deadlines is easy. But Dr. Dyer's reminder to be present has helped me stay grounded.

When I work with clients, I am fully present and give them my full attention. It's not about multitasking or thinking about the next thing on my to-do list; it's about listening and engaging in the conversation. This has made a huge difference in the relationships I've built with my clients. They can feel that I'm truly invested in their success, and that's something that sets us apart.

The same goes for my team. Being present in my interactions with them —during a team meeting or a quick chat—helps build trust and connection. They know I'm there for them and that I'm not just going through the motions. It's about creating a work environment where people feel seen and heard; that all starts with being present.

I've tried to implement this in my daily routine by setting aside "presence moments" throughout the day. These are times when I deliberately pause whatever I'm doing and focus entirely on the person or task at hand. Whether it's a 10-minute check-in with a team member or a few minutes to connect with a client, these moments help me stay grounded and connected.

I've also learned to appreciate the little things. It's easy to get so wrapped up in the bigger picture that you forget to enjoy the journey. But being present means finding joy in the small wins—the positive feedback from a client, the excitement in a team member's voice when they achieve something great, or even just a quiet moment of reflection at the end of a busy day. These are the moments that make all the hard work worth it.

Balancing Belief & Skepticism

As much as I've taken Dr. Dyer's teachings to heart, I also believe in maintaining a balance between belief and skepticism. Not everything he says resonates with me, and that's okay. I think it's important to take what works for you and leave the rest.

For me, it's about practical application. How do these ideas fit into my real-world experience? How do they help me navigate the day-to-day challenges of running a business? If something doesn't resonate, I don't force it. But when something like the power of intention or being present does click, I run with it.

This approach has allowed me to stay true to myself while still being open to new ideas. It's about finding that balance between embracing what works and being okay with letting go of what doesn't. And in the end, that's what has made my businesses more authentic and aligned with my personal values.

Keeping it Real

I don't claim to be an expert on everything Dr. Dyer taught, but these two ideas—setting intentions and being present—have resonated with me and shaped how I approach my businesses. They're simple concepts, but they've had a big impact.

Ultimately, what matters to me is that I'm building businesses that align with my values and positively impact the people I work with and the clients we serve. Dr. Dyer's teachings have helped me stay focused on what's important; I'm grateful for that.

As I continue to grow Cloversy and The Six-Figure Chicks, I'll remember these principles. They remind me to stay true to my intentions and to be present in the moment—two things that have made all the difference in my journey so far.

Embracing the Journey

One final thought that ties all of this together is embracing the journey. Building a business—or two—takes time, effort, and a lot of perseverance. There are ups and downs, successes and challenges, but what keeps me going is the mindset that this is all part of the journey.

Dr. Dyer often spoke about the importance of enjoying the process rather than just focusing on the end goal. I try to remind myself of this every day. It's easy to get caught up in the hustle and forget to appreciate how far you've come and your progress.

Whether it's celebrating a new client win, seeing a team member grow into their role, or simply knowing that we're making a difference in someone's life, these are the moments that make the journey worthwhile.

They remind us that, at the end of the day, it's not just about the destination but about how we get there.

So, while I may not agree with everything Dr. Dyer taught, the ideas that resonate with me have had a lasting impact. They've helped shape who I am as a business owner and continue guiding me as I navigate this journey. And for that, I'm thankful.

~ Mel C

MEL CARR

About Mel Carr: Mel Carr stands as a testament to the essence of profound introspection and self-awareness. She consistently dedicates time to understanding herself and those around her, seeking out beauty, meaning, and purpose in every facet of life. With an inherent ability to perceive what's "above and beyond" mere limitations, Mel's life resonates deeply with gratitude, humor, playfulness, and a graceful acceptance of the uncontrollable. Her innate curiosity allows her to unearth fresh and startling ideas, enabling her to engage wholeheartedly with life's mysteries and the sacred elements it holds.

As the esteemed Founder and Director of Cloversy, Mel possesses an uncanny understanding of time management and decision-making processes, irrespective of the content or environment. She's an emblem of organizational prowess, always at the forefront, ensuring every business need is met with precision and care. Mel's adeptness in resolving conflicts, enhancing brainstorming sessions, and fostering creativity sets her apart in the industry. She's ever attentive to customer feedback, ensuring prompt responses and resolutions to their queries. Infusing businesses with a fresh outlook and innovative ideas, Mel Carr is the catalyst that many organizations need to transcend their limitations. If you're looking to elevate your business, connecting with Mel is a promising pathway to boundless potential.

Author's Website: *www.Cloversy.com*

Book Series Website: *www.TheBookOfMentors.com*

"THERE IS NO WAY TO HAPPINESS, HAPPINESS IS THE WAY."

~ DR. WAYNE DYER

HONORING DR. WAYNE DYER

DR. ONIKA SHIRLEY

MANIFESTING YOUR POTENTIAL

"Be miserable. Or motivate yourself. Whatever has to be done, it's always your choice."
~ Dr. Wayne Dyer

The Power of Actions Speak Volumes

As a young mother at the age of fifteen, faced with the reality of pregnancy and motherhood at such a tender age, I found myself at a crossroads. The weight of responsibility fell squarely on my shoulders as I navigated the challenges of single motherhood, becoming the caregiver to my daughter at just sixteen-years-old. In those early days, as I grappled with the consequences of my choices and the mistakes that led me to that point, I realized the profound truth that Wayne Dyer often spoke of—the importance of taking responsibility for our own lives and decisions.

It was a pivotal moment of growth and self-realization, a journey that taught me the invaluable lesson of owning up to my past, embracing my present, and shaping my future with intention and accountability. In sharing my story, I hope to inspire and mentor others, not just in the realm of parenthood, but in all aspects of life, emphasizing the transformative power of personal responsibility and the freedom that comes with taking charge of our own destinies.

As we journey through life, we are confronted with a myriad of choices and decisions that shape our path and define our reality. It is in these moments of choice that we hold immense power—the power to create our own destiny, to shape our future with purpose and intention. Each decision we make, every action we take, is a reflection of our innermost desires and beliefs, guiding us toward the life we envision for ourselves. By taking responsibility for our choices and embracing the power of intention, we unlock the key to unlocking our full potential and living a life of authenticity and fulfillment. Let us embark on this transformative journey together, embracing the inherent power within us to shape our destinies and manifest our dreams into reality.

Let us no longer dwell in the shadows of blame or regret, but, instead, let us step into the light of accountability and empowerment. By acknowledging our past mistakes and taking ownership of our actions, we free ourselves from the chains of victimhood and open the door to true personal growth and transformation. With each conscious choice we make, we affirm our commitment to living a life of purpose and integrity, guided by the unwavering force of intention.

It is through this mindful awareness and dedication to self-responsibility that we can truly experience the profound beauty of creating our own reality and shaping our destiny according to our deepest desires. Embrace the power of intention, take hold of the reins of your life, and watch as the universe aligns to support you on your journey toward a life of authenticity, fulfillment, and joy.

Eight Actionable Things You Could Do Now to Take You Steps Farther on Your Current Journey:

1. **Reflect on Your Choices:** Take time to reflect on the choices you have made in the past and their impact on your life. Acknowledge both the positive and negative outcomes and use this self-awareness to guide your future decisions.

2. **Practice Mindfulness:** Cultivate mindfulness in your daily life by being present in the moment and aware of your thoughts, emotions, and actions. Mindfulness can help you make more conscious choices aligned with your values and intentions.

3. **Set Clear Intentions:** Define your goals and aspirations with clarity and purpose. Write down your intentions and revisit them regularly to stay focused and motivated on your journey toward personal growth and fulfillment.

4. **Take Ownership:** Embrace responsibility for your actions and their consequences. Avoid blaming others or external circumstances for your challenges, and, instead, empower yourself by recognizing your role in shaping your own reality.

5. **Seek Support:** Surround yourself with positive influences and seek mentorship from those who inspire and uplift you. Connect with like-minded individuals who share your values and goals and lean on their guidance and encouragement when needed.

6. **Embrace the Growth Mindset:** Adopt a growth mindset that views challenges as opportunities for learning and development. Embrace setbacks as valuable lessons that propel you forward and cultivate resilience in the face of adversity.

7. **Practice Self-Care:** Prioritize self-care and well-being as essential components of personal responsibility. Nurture your physical, emotional, and mental health through practices such as exercise, meditation, self-reflection, and seeking professional support when needed.

8. **Take Action:** Turn your intentions into tangible actions by setting achievable goals and taking consistent steps toward their realization. Break down larger tasks into manageable steps, celebrate your progress, and stay committed to your journey of personal empowerment and growth.

In reflecting on my journey as a teen parent, living independently since the age of sixteen and successfully raising my children to achieve their educational milestones, I realize that I have unknowingly applied the principles outlined in the eight actionable steps. From taking on the role of a responsible parent at a young age to prioritizing self-care and personal growth while balancing work and family commitments, I have consistently set clear intentions, embraced challenges as opportunities for learning and development, and sought support from mentors and a positive community.

By owning my choices and actions, fostering a growth mindset, and consistently taking steps toward my goals, I have demonstrated resilience, determination, and a strong sense of personal responsibility in navigating life's challenges and shaping my reality. As I continue this journey of self-empowerment and growth, I am inspired to further cultivate mindfulness, set new intentions, and take deliberate actions aligned with my values and aspirations to create a fulfilling and purpose-driven life for myself and my family.

Reflective Questions

1. How can I apply the insights gained from reflecting on my past choices and their impact on my life to make more intentional decisions moving forward?

2. In what ways can I incorporate mindfulness practices into my daily routine to cultivate greater self-awareness, clarity, and purpose in aligning my actions with my values and intentions?

3. What specific steps can I take today to demonstrate a deeper commitment to taking ownership of my life, embracing personal responsibility, and actively pursuing my goals and aspirations with courage and determination?

"Your life has a purpose. Your story is important. Your dreams count. Your voice matters. You were born to make an impact."
~ Dr. Wayne Dyer

In conclusion, the journey of self-discovery, personal growth, and empowerment is a continuous process that requires reflection, intentionality, and action. Throughout my work of raising my children, I continued to pursue my education journey, starting from graduating high school to achieving an associate's, bachelor's, master's, and even a doctorate degree.

By embracing the principles outlined in the eight actionable steps and drawing inspiration from profound quotes like the one by Wayne Dyer, we can cultivate a mindset of responsibility, resilience, and purpose in navigating life's challenges and shaping our reality. Whether it be as a teen parent, a young individual living independently, or a seasoned professional guiding others toward success, the power of self-awareness, intention setting, and deliberate action can propel us toward our goals and aspirations. As we continue to apply these transformative principles in our lives, we unlock our fullest potential, create meaningful impact, and inspire others to do the same.

Through my journey of balancing parenthood, education, and personal growth, I have learned the importance of perseverance, dedication, and a strong sense of purpose. Each degree I earned symbolizes not only academic achievement but also a testament to my unwavering commitment to self-improvement and lifelong learning.

As I reflect on the challenges and triumphs that have shaped my path, I am reminded that true success is not solely measured by degrees or titles but by the resilience, determination, and growth mindset that we cultivate along the way. By embracing the principles of responsibility, intentionality, and action, I have not only achieved academic milestones but also nurtured a sense of fulfillment, purpose, and empowerment that continues to guide me on my journey toward personal and professional excellence.

As I look toward the future with optimism and gratitude, I am inspired to continue applying these transformative principles in all aspects of my life, knowing that the possibilities for growth and impact are endless when we embrace the power of self-awareness, intention, and action.

DR. ONIKA SHIRLEY

About Dr. Onika L. Shirley: Dr. Onika L. Shirley is the Founder and CEO of Action Speaks Volume, Inc. She is a Procrastination Strategist and Behavior Change Expert and known for building unshakable confidence; stopping procrastination, and getting your dreams out of your head into your life. She is a Master Storyteller, International Speaker, Serves in Global Ministry, International Bestselling Author, International Award Recipient, Serial Entrepreneur, and Global Philanthropist impacting lives in the USA, Africa, India, and Pakistan.

Dr. O is a Motivational Speaker and Christian Counselor. Dr. Onika is the Founder and Director of Action Speaks Volume Orphanage Home and Sewing School in Telangana State, India, and the Founder and Director of Action Speaks Volume Sewing School in Khanewal and Shankot, Pakistan. She founded, operated, and visited an Orphanage home in Tuni, India, for four years, and she supported widows in Tuni, India.

She is the founder of Empowering Eight Inner Circle, ASV C.A.R.E.S, ASV Next Level Living Program, and P6 Solutions and Consulting. She has served for 13 years as a therapeutic foster parent. Of all the things Dr. O does, she is most proud of her profound faith in Christ and her opportunity to serve the body of Christ globally.

Author's Website: *www.ActionSpeaksVolumes.com*

Book Series Website: *www.TheBookOfMentors.com*

RITU CHOPRA

THE TRIAD OF LEADERSHIP

"*When you change the way you look at things,
the things you look at change.*"
~ **Dr. Wayne Dyer**

In today's rapidly evolving world, leadership has transcended traditional paradigms to encompass a complex interplay of qualities in the 21st Century. Among these, self-awareness, charisma, and consciousness are foundational pillars and transformative forces upon which modern leaders build their success. The well-known author, Wayne Dyer emphasized the importance of self-awareness; it remains the timeless quality of leaders of any generation.

This topic delves into the significance of these attributes, their interconnections, and their profound impact on effective leadership in the contemporary landscape, inspiring and motivating leaders of communities and organizations of all sizes to embrace these qualities for personal and professional growth. This leadership triad is like an anchor of strength in our modern times.

Let's discuss these pillars, their interconnectedness and power in detail:

Self-Awareness

The Keystone of Leadership, "Self-awareness," often regarded as the cornerstone of effective leadership, encapsulates an understanding of one's emotions, strengths, weaknesses, and motivations. In the context of leadership, self-awareness empowers individuals to navigate challenges with clarity and authenticity. Leaders with a keen self-awareness are better equipped to make sound decisions, communicate effectively, and foster meaningful relationships within their communities and organizations.

Due to their increased emotional intelligence, self-aware leaders can also empathize with the perspectives and experiences of others. They acknowledge their limitations and continuously seek improvement so that they can inspire growth and development within their organization.

Charisma

The Magnetic Force of Influence is a charisma one possesses, often characterized as a compelling charm or magnetic appeal, and is instrumental in shaping a leader's influence and impact. While charisma may be innate to some extent, it is also a skill that can be cultivated and refined through conscious effort. Charismatic leaders possess confidence, enthusiasm, and authenticity that captivate and inspire those around them.

One of the defining traits of charismatic leaders is their ability to articulate and mobilize others around a compelling vision. Through persuasive communication and infectious enthusiasm, they rally support, build coalitions, and galvanize action. Their charismatic nature enables them to build rapport and collaborate effectively with various members of society.

Truly charismatic leaders align their words with actions, demonstrating integrity, authenticity, and a genuine commitment to their vision and values. By embracing these qualities, leaders earn trust and loyalty, fostering enduring relationships and sustainable success. When charisma lacks substance or integrity, it can be superficial and fleeting.

Consciousness

The evolution of leadership consciousness, often described as an elevated state of awareness and mindfulness, represents the evolution of leadership in modern times. Beyond mere self-awareness, consciousness encompasses a deeper understanding of interconnectedness, purpose, and the broader impact of one's actions. Conscious leaders recognize their responsibility not only to their organizations but also to society and the planet as a whole.

Conscious leadership is rooted in empathy, compassion, and ethical integrity. Leaders who operate from a place of consciousness prioritize the well-being of all they touch and impact, considering the long-term implications of their decisions on people, the planet, and prosperity.

Furthermore, conscious leaders foster a culture of inclusivity, diversity, and equity, recognizing every individual's worth and dignity. Through empathy and inclusivity, every team member feels valued and involved in the leadership process.

More importantly, conscious leadership extends beyond the confines of traditional hierarchies, embracing collaborative and decentralized approaches to decision-making and problem-solving. By empowering others, nurturing collective intelligence, and fostering a culture of learning and innovation, conscious leaders catalyze positive change and pave the way for sustainable growth. This perspective instills a sense of hope and optimism in the audience, encouraging them to adopt conscious leadership practices.

The Interconnectedness of Self-awareness, Charisma, & Consciousness

While self-awareness, charisma, and consciousness represent distinct dimensions of leadership, they are interconnected and mutually reinforcing. Self-awareness forms the foundation upon which charisma and consciousness are built, enabling leaders to cultivate authenticity, integrity, and empathy. Charisma catalyzes influence and inspiration, amplifying the impact of conscious leadership by engaging and mobilizing others toward a compelling and shared vision. Consciousness, in turn, enriches self-awareness and charisma by expanding leaders' perspectives, deepening their empathy, and aligning their actions with broader societal and environmental imperatives.

The Outcome of Interconnectedness of the Triad

The triad of conscious leadership for modern times in our global village draws attention to the compelling and shared vision for humanity, the people, the planet, and prosperity. A compelling vision and the ability to mobilize others toward its realization are hallmarks of effective leadership, shaping the trajectory of organizations, movements, and societies.

A compelling vision is a guiding light, illuminating the path forward amidst uncertainty and adversity. When coupled with the power to mobilize others, it becomes a force capable of catalyzing innovation, fostering collaboration, and achieving remarkable outcomes. It inspires hearts and minds, galvanizes collective action, and drives transformation. History abounds with examples of visionary leaders who, through their ability to articulate a compelling vision and mobilize others, have sparked movements, toppled regimes, and ushered in eras of progress and prosperity. Our potential to cultivate this ability becomes increasingly crucial as we face the challenges of the 21st Century.

Wayne Dyer, a renowned self-help author and mentor, left behind a legacy of profound insights and inspiring quotes. *"Change the way you look at things and the things you look at change."* This quote reflects Dyer's belief in the transformative power of perception. It highlights the idea that our perspective shapes our reality, and by shifting our mindset, we can alter our experiences and outcomes.

Expanding one's worldview by seeking different perspectives and viewpoints is crucial for leaders in today's interconnected and diverse world, fostering a culture of inclusivity and belonging within organizations. When leaders actively seek diverse perspectives, they signal their teams that all voices are valued and respected. This, in turn, encourages team members to contribute their unique insights and ideas, leading to more creative and innovative solutions.

The terms DEI, DEIB, JDEI, etc., have become common in most business leaders' vocabulary. Inclusivity is not just a national concept but a global phenomenon nowadays. For 21st-Century leaders, it's vital to understand the dynamics of the planet and humanity first.

It is evident that inclusive leadership strengthens team dynamics and enhances organizational performance and adaptability in an increasingly globalized and interconnected world. This approach promotes critical thinking and open-mindedness so people's creativity can flow in the age of technological innovations. A conscious, heart-centered, self-aware leader is sure to succeed in his/her mission and gain support.

Leaders must cultivate curiosity, humility, and openness to learning from others. They should be willing to challenge their assumptions and biases and embrace discomfort as a catalyst for growth and understanding. A continuous learning culture and self-reflection encourage diversity and value diverse perspectives. The use of technology and digital platforms to access diverse perspectives and viewpoints is common these days.

Here are key actions we can take from the triad of leadership to empower our persona and perspectives:

1. **Cultivate Awareness:** The first step in changing how we look at things is cultivating awareness of our current perspectives and beliefs. Reflect on your thoughts, attitudes, and interpretations of events. Notice any recurring patterns or biases that may be influencing your perception.

2. **Practice Mindfulness:** Engage in mindfulness to become more present and attuned to the present moment. Mindfulness meditation, deep breathing exercises, or pausing to observe your surroundings can aid in gaining a deeper understanding of your emotions and thoughts.

3. **Challenge Limiting Beliefs:** Identify any limiting beliefs or negative thought patterns that may hold you back. Ask yourself whether these beliefs are based on objective reality or subjective interpretations. Reframe these beliefs more powerfully by seeking evidence to the contrary.

4. **Seek Different Perspectives:** Expand your worldview by seeking different perspectives and viewpoints. Be open to new ideas and

experiences by speaking with people from diverse backgrounds and reading books that challenge your assumptions.

5. **Practice Gratitude:** Highlight the positive aspects of your life and experiences by cultivating an attitude of gratitude. Gratitude shifts your focus away from scarcity and negativity toward abundance and appreciation, leading to a more optimistic and positive outlook.

6. **Embrace Challenges as Opportunities:** Reframe challenges as learning opportunities instead of hindrances. Adopt a growth mindset that embraces failure as a natural part of the learning process and sees setbacks as opportunities to pivot and evolve.

7. **Visualize Success:** Use the power of visualization to imagine yourself achieving your goals and aspirations. Visualizing success helps clarify your objectives and instills confidence and motivation to pursue them with determination and resilience.

8. **Practice Self-Compassion:** Show yourself kindness and compassion, especially during difficult times. Embrace your challenges with the same kindness and understanding you would give to a friend. Adopt and embrace self-care activities that nourish your body, mind, and spirit.

In conclusion, self-awareness, charisma, and consciousness emerge as the bedrock of leadership in modern times, shaping the character, influence, and impact of individuals in positions of authority. By cultivating these qualities, leaders can navigate complexity with clarity, inspire action with authenticity, and drive positive change with purpose. As we navigate the myriad challenges and opportunities of the 21st Century, embracing the triad of self-awareness, charisma, and consciousness offers a transformative pathway toward enlightened leadership and collective flourishing.

RITU CHOPRA

About Ritu Chopra: Ritu Chopra, a technologist by profession, an author, TV show host, award-winning film producer, a certified leadership coach, and international speaker who is on her spiritual journey.

With 25+ years of experience in Fortune 500 companies serving in IT operations, information security in global financial, & health care industries, Ritu now mentors and coaches emerging leaders to achieve their 'Personal Mastery.'

Ritu is the Founder of Lead My Way, a not-for-profit organization, and she is a passionate advocate of women and youth leadership and empowerment initiatives.

Author Website: *www.RituChopra.com*

Book Series Website: *www.TheBookOfMentors.com*

HONORING DR. WAYNE DYER

SALLY WURR

NOT EVERYONE CAN BE A MENTOR—CHOOSE WISELY

Mentorship is a valuable resource on the journey to personal and professional growth. Figuring out how best to utilize the experience and expertise of your mentor to maximize your potential and achieve your goals should be your main objective.

In order to get everything that you need out of your mentor, there are some basic steps that you have to understand and utilize.

The first step is to establish clear objectives with your mentor. Identify the specific areas where you need help and improvement. This could be for career advancement, leadership skills, or personal development. When you set clear objectives, you provide your mentor with a road map of what you hope to achieve; it allows them to tailor their guidance to your needs.

You must also build a foundation based on trust. With open and honest communication between both parties, you foster this trust and become better at actively listening to your mentor. You must be receptive to constructive criticism because one of the biggest hurdles mentees have is not accepting constructive criticism. Your mentor's expertise and experience are valuable resources.

Make sure that you're asking thoughtful questions and asking for their perspective on the different situations that you may run into. You can then utilize their knowledge to gain insight and learn from their successes and their failures. Additionally, look for opportunities to learn together, such as attending events, workshops, or conferences. These shared experiences will strengthen your bond and provide valuable networking opportunities.

You must also maintain regular and consistent communication to maximize the benefits of mentorship. Sometimes, it's best to set up a schedule for meetings or check-ins that works for both of you. This way, you're going to receive the consistent guidance and support that you need to succeed.

Feedback is a critical component of mentorship. Your mentors should provide guidance and insight based on their experience and expertise. It is essential that you act on their feedback and implement their suggestions. Be proactive and take the initiative to apply their advice and explore new opportunities. By demonstrating your commitment to growth and improvement, you showcase your dedication to the mentor and to your own development. If you are unsure, ask for examples or further guidance.

Sometimes your mentor can be an excellent source of networking opportunities. You can leverage their connections to expand your professional network. By attending industry events or joining relevant professional groups, you can meet like-minded individuals. Networking allows you to gain exposure, learn from others, and discover new opportunities that can propel your career forward.

Finding a mentor who firmly believes in the power of encouragement in your abilities is important. Your mentor should inspire and motivate you to overcome obstacles and tap into your potential. Your mentor should nurture a positive mindset and self-confidence through consistent encouragement. By doing so it can help you develop a resilient attitude and conquer challenges on your journey to success.

It is important that you set clear and specific goals for yourself for the short term, as well as long term in order to provide you direction and purpose. You need to be accountable and regularly track your progress toward these goals. Your mentor can help you figure out what's the best way for you to be able to do so.

Each person must accept responsibility for their growth. Mentors serve as guides, but it is ultimately up to the mentees to take action and apply the guidance received. You must make conscious choices aligned with your values and embrace your personal accountability. That is how to create a life of fulfillment and purpose.

Part of harnessing all these traits is that they extend beyond your sphere. It creates a ripple effect that influences the people around you and others that you may mentor in your future. By embracing the skills that you learn through your mentor for personal growth, you will naturally spread that knowledge and wisdom and inspiration to those around you.

As a recap for finding a great mentor, please remember these goals:

- Develop a clear understanding of your goals and what you wish to gain.
- Look for a mentor that has the knowledge, expertise, and skills you need to learn.
- Develop a relationship built on trust and compatibility.
- Understand your potential mentor's background and achievements.
- Express admiration for your mentor's success and work. Be clear about why you chose them to be your mentor.
- Be respectful of their time and availability.
- Show enthusiasm and commitment to your growth.
- Have a clear understanding of your expectations.
- Discuss the frequency of meetings and track your progress.
- Be gracious and express your gratitude for their guidance and support.
- Be teachable! When you mentor shares ideas, follow through and apply them.
- Pay it forward and become a mentor yourself!

Remember that finding the right mentor may take time and effort, but a strong mentorship can be significant to help propel you further in your career.

While finding a good mentor is refreshing, there are also things you need to look out for. Not everyone is cut out to be a mentor!

Mentorship can be a noble endeavor, but it's important to recognize that not everyone is cut out to be a mentor. Effective mentorship requires a unique blend of qualities, experiences, and skills that not all individuals possess.

One of the fundamental reasons not everyone can be a mentor is the requirement for substantial experience and expertise in a particular field or area. Mentors are expected to provide guidance, share insights, and offer valuable advice based on their own experiences. Without this expertise, mentors may struggle to provide the guidance and knowledge that mentees seek.

Affective mentorship also demands a high degree of empathy and patience. Mentors must be able to understand the challenges and concerns of their mentees, even if those challenges differ from their own experiences. Empathy allows mentors to connect with their mentees on a personal level and offer support that is tailored to their individual needs. Patience is equally crucial as mentorship often involves helping mentees through setbacks and obstacles, which can require time and persistence.

Mentorship is a communication-driven relationship. Mentors should be good listeners, able to actively engage with their mentees, ask questions, and provide constructive feedback. Without strong communication skills, the mentorship process can break down, leading to misunderstandings and frustrated parties.

Mentorship should be a selfless act focused on the growth and development of the mentee. If the person is primarily motivated by personal gain, recognition, or self-interest, they may not be the right fit for a mentorship role.

A mentor's role is to offer constructive feedback, encouragement, and support. If they tend to be overly critical, unsupportive, or dismissive of others' ideas and efforts, their approach may not align with the nurturing and empowering nature of mentorship.

While your mentor's expertise is valuable, don't limit yourself to their perspective alone. Be open to different viewpoints and approaches. Diversity of thought can spark creativity and help you see problems from different angles.

Another important part of mentorship is to regularly assess your progress toward your goals. Are you making strides in the right direction? If not, you need to discuss them and together develop a strategy that pushes you where you need to go.

Personally, I look at mentors as "guiding lights" on my path to success. My active participation is the key to making the most of the relationship.

Embrace the mentorship journey as a valuable opportunity for learning, self-improvement, and achieving your aspirations.

SALLY WURR

About Sally Wurr: Sally Wurr is an international speaker and multi-book author.

Sally is known as the "Storm Whisperer" because her message is about how to prepare for life's storms. Each person has trials and tragedies, but it is how we react to those events that help us grow and survive in our business and personal activities.

By sharing her expertise with stories, she teaches you how to embrace change and how to face life's struggles head-on. Simply put, she likes to teach others how to problem solve.

Sally embraces the knowledge that those who can must be the ones that do. She shares her stories so that others can find their true purpose.

In addition to writing and speaking, Sally is the President and Founder of SW Insurance Corp. She has helped thousands of CEOs develop employee benefits programs to attain and retain employees. It is her problem-solving and attention to detail that have made her successful in this arena for many years.

Author's Website: *www.SallyWurr.com*

Book Series Website: *www.TheBookOfMentors.com*

SARAH LEE

YOU ARE PERFECT JUST THE WAY YOU ARE

You are perfect, just the way you are... (but keep working on it, too). You have the power.

Here's what Lao Tzu said in verse 29: "You think you can take over the Universe and improve it? I do not believe it can be done."

Everything under heaven is a sacred vessel and cannot be controlled. Trying to control leads to ruin. Trying to grasp, we lose.

"Allow your life to unfold naturally.
Know that it too, is a vessel of perfection."
~ Dr. Wayne Dyer

Not to get side tracked, but many do not know that Lao Tzu was not a person, it was a concept. Lao Tzu was a group of authors, in China, who had some wisdom, experience, and ideas that were collected and put in one place, a series of texts and attributed to Lao Tzu. Wayne Dyer read a lot of ancient wisdom from different cultures, and used meditation to learn lessons in an even deeper manner by communing with the universe.

This was also true for many other great thinkers and inventors like Tesla, and Einstein, for example. They used meditation to learn things in the Quantum realm, and then tested it in the "real world," the world we see and think of as real.

This idea of communicating with the Universe is now a part of Quantum Mechanics, which is a subset of Quantum Physics, a topic that many of you have never studied and or completely kept up with. I will refer to those ideas today, but I promise to keep this interesting.

I, personally, am often quoted suggesting that people read a book, first published in the 1990s, called, "The Holographic Universe." It was written by two scientists, who were the editors in a premiere physics journal. They had a theory that things that humans once thought of as "Hocus Pocus" are actually ideas that can be tested and proven out as actual science.

They had, and I believe still have, the same point of view on this topic. The same point of view that I have now, but that book opened my mind. The first time I read *The Holographic Universe* was years before I studied meditation in person with Living Legends and gurus like Sri Sri Ravi Shankar, who worked for years on meditation with the Beatles, and the now world famous Chinese Dr. Sha from San Francisco, who is a medical doctor but also is a renowned healer and guru.

My awareness of this book was also before I became a certified expert in guided Medical Meditation for hospitals and healing, and before I became a licensed hypnotherapist.

In the years after I learned of these ideas, I also became a noted behavioral and business expert on *Think and Grow Rich.* While I was reading *Holographic Universe*, I worked as an intern at UCLA's Neuropsychiatric doing behavioral training for nonverbal autistic children. I was thinking very deeply about how people really actually communicate with one another and why some things stick to us and others do not.

A Few Things I Learned from the Book:

1.   The brain, while useful, is not what's controlling your movements or thoughts.

2. Empty space is not empty. It is likely connected (think String Theory) and this was proven by a Yale study, that your heart reacts to other people's energy, which is commonly called intuition but it is not intuition at all. The space between things is actually physically connected but invisible to the eye. So, often you are actually feeling something that is or was happening—as a signal from the person you want to communicate with. It is not just a guess.

The idea of the book was maybe like a hologram—all of the parts are contained in the whole. Meaning, for non-science geeks, maybe each cell in your body knows everything that you know, and can do all of the work that each part of your body can do.

This was revolutionary at the time. It is now almost wholly accepted as science.

The reason I bring this up is two-fold.

1. Just because you do not understand something does not mean it is not working and happening for, with, or to you.

2. What was once considered "New Age Belief" is now accepted as science.

I do not understand gravity, on this planet or otherwise, and yet I am not going to jump off a bridge to test to see if it works. (Physics has found examples of gravity following different principles now, in outer space, even principles that do not work how science once thought it did.

Many animals, including humans, are known to have a collective memory—flies, crabs, monkeys, fleas, bees, ants, to name a few. The idea, scientifically, is that animals not only teach each other things but, after a period of time, the animals in the entire area will accept the idea as fact, even if it is not true for them. They will stop questioning the truth of something. Interesting, isn't it?

Humans share information with each other via their DNA. Mothers have not only all of her own eggs but all of her unborn daughters' eggs in her when she is born. If you are a female, your mother is always a part of you and they are still trying to figure out what this means for humans.

But Wayne Dyer wanted to know more... And when he learned something new, he taught it. Just like many of the great thinkers in life.

With the observer effect, it is now understood that humans can change reality based on the energy they put into something and the thoughts and words they use while observing a possible outcome.

While we once believed that we were small in the universe, we now know for sure that we are co-creating with the universe quite literally.

Our thoughts and choices matter. Our intentions matter maybe most, as that is what is most likely what is *read* by the universe as to what *we want*. That was what was in the book, *Think and Grow Rich*, and those ideas are contained in Wayne Dyer's work as well.

In the 1960s, a female biologist asserted that it was not us controlling our lives and choices but it was bacteria. She was laughed at. Progress was made in 2005, when a Nobel Prize was given to scientists, which helped us understand the role of bacteria in the gut. The original scientist recently, in 2020, won a Nobel prize for that research on bacteria as well and it is now accepted science.

Bacteria eat your food. Our cells do not eat any of the food you eat; we eat the waste from the bacteria. Our human cells cannot take in food in the form that we consume and digest it. So, there are theories now that bacteria and human cells "talk" somehow and that is what makes us do a lot of the things we "like to do."

Wayne Dyer started to intuit a lot of this when he was alive. He started to speak of it as programming cells and your mind through nightly self-hypnosis. He felt if we were already programmed by everything we ever experienced, saw, or felt and if some of that programming also comes from "outside of us" as well as our parents' DNA and genes, what could we do to determine our own lives?

At that time, he did not know the things I just explained to you. He guessed. But it all turned out to be truly how things work.

I always pay extra attention to someone that seems to know how to get things to work for them, things that other people find mysterious or unidentified. Wayne Dyer was one of those people.

You do not have to be a science geek to get the benefit of what Wayne taught. You can look him up on YouTube and get a lot of his wisdom for free.

I believe that Wayne Dyer understood that he, in his own life, was an acting force and the greatest part of that force was his energy and belief. I teach classes on this through my program, "Fertile Soil of the Mind— How to Prepare your Mind for Success,"™ where we talk about the science of mindset and give you helpful, actionable tools to help you get ready to learn anything new and help you change your own mindset.

Wayne knew the power of change. He knew the power of decision and the power of dreaming and creating your life in another realm, if nothing else to 1) communicate with the Universe and 2) to tell the Universe what exactly you want.

Bob Proctor used to always say, "If you can see it in your mind, you can hold it in your hand."

At Fertile Soil, we take it one step further.

In order to shift, in order to have something new, you must create it in your mind, for sure—but in the act of creating the space for it, in both physical reality and with your third eye, **you can create the energy for someone else to receive it and to join you.** This is part of both manifestation and creation, as well as being part of enrollment.

"In order to have something you have never had before, you must become the person who can do that thing you want to do."
~ Earl Nightingale

We teach that the step of not just thinking about it, wishing for it or wanting it, but really tediously actually building it in your mind, is essential to creation. That is why dream boards work, as well as manifestation. You only can create what you are an energetic match for. But you can tune yourself like a tuning fork to vibrate differently and do things like protect yourself from negative people, negative results and energy, and also to create a signal so others are drawn to you, to help you achieve your expected and chosen results.

In fact, we assert that this is the only way anything ever is created. All else is folly. All the other steps are just very important parts of the whole journey to get there, but they are not the whole. And like all great wisdom, in any field, you can do 99% of it right and one big part of it wrong, and it won't work for you. That doesn't mean it doesn't work. It might mean you need more or better information, as T. Harv Eker would say.

That's why you read books like these on the greats from the greats. Most overcomers know something you might not know, else you would have already overcome the issue yourself.

Thank you once again for spending some time with us today!

We appreciate you. Consider following us for more @coachmeacademy on Instagram and *www.Facebook.com/CoachMeSaraLee*

SARAH LEE

About Sarah Lee, MBA: A brilliant educational psychologist and leadership expert by education, Sarah Lee is the innovative author of *Rock Soup - An Innovational Idea in Leadership.* By profession, Sarah has been teaching financial literacy for the last 15 years using her own firm as a platform. She is a full-service financial advisor and manager of her own Securities Branch of a national firm. She has networked with 100 Brokers all over the US. Sarah has an MBA in Finance and Social Impact and is 14 months shy of a Ph.D. in Educational Leadership. She is also the founder of multiple other companies and brands; some sold for profit, some she learned from, and some she consulted on for other businesses. She is now mostly currently focused on her production company with her husband, MONEY MENTOR, LLC™.

She has been advocating and speaking on large issues like financial literacy, literacy mindset, clean water, and service to the world (hunger, water issues, poverty, and literacy) for her entire life. At nine-years-old, she said, "I would like to host a consumer reports show, where I would interview local business owners and see how I could highlight them while giving them ways to give back and make a difference." That led to a life of public speaking, running endowments, and working with local universities on educational issues. She developed her world-famous business philosophy during this time: "Business is just like Rock Soup…" @coachmeSarahLee, @moneymentormethod; Instagram: @moneymentorcompany, @coachmeacademy. For Money Tips, you can text the words "MONEYMENTOR" to 55444 for a free gift or visit our webpage: linktr.ee/MoneyMentorMethod.

Author's Website: *www.MoneyMentorFreeGift.com*

Book Series Website: *www.TheBookOfMentors.com*

HONORING DR. WAYNE DYER

"WHEN YOU DANCE, YOUR PURPOSE IS NOT TO GET TO A CERTAIN PLACE ON THE FLOOR. IT'S TO ENJOY EACH STEP ALONG THE WAY."

~ DR. WAYNE DYER

STACEY HALL

A MENTOR'S PATH: FAITH, LEADERSHIP, & POSITIVITY

Mentorship has been one of the most profound and transformative roles in my life. Beyond simply fulfilling its responsibilities, it's been both a privilege and an opportunity to lead others toward reaching their fullest potential while also growing myself. After sharing my journey in these books, mentorship has served as my compass throughout—from mothering my daughters to professional dentistry practice management, employer responsibility responsibilities, community outreach initiatives, and volunteerism roles; it remains a testament to faith as an unyielding strength of mine.

Mentor & Mentee Roles

In my experience, one of the hallmarks of successful mentorship relationships is their reciprocal nature. While I've had the honor of mentoring many over time, I also benefitted greatly from being mentored myself! Effective mentoring relationships require mutual respect, trust, and an aim of personal and professional growth as key ingredients of their foundation.

My journey began with my parents as my initial mentors. They instilled within me the values of hard work, perseverance, and faith—values that continue to influence every aspect of my life today. Later in my career journey, I encountered mentors who helped develop my technical dental abilities and also encouraged me to view patients holistically as individuals rather than simply symptoms to treat. Not only were these mentors people who inspired me to strive for excellence in my work and practice, but many of them became more than just mentors and acquaintances—some even peers, colleagues, and my closest allies.

Faith is our Guide

Faith has always been at the core of my life, providing strength, guidance, and an overall sense of direction and purpose. When serving as a mentor myself, my faith serves as the cornerstone for leading and supporting others. Mentorship, to me, extends far beyond professional achievements—it involves supporting growth while inspiring individuals to realize their full potential with honesty and kindness.

Although my professional path has not led me to learn more about the life and journey of Dr. Wayne Dyer's teachings, I've learned that some of his teachings align with my beliefs and experience, which resonated deeply with me, particularly his belief that our positive thoughts do shape our reality. I can attest firsthand how positivity influences those around us—it has more significant influence than we can even begin to measure, and that encourages others to adopt similar mindsets, as evidenced by my experiences and observations. Furthermore, his ideas surrounding frequency positively aligned closely with my faith-based experiences, which helped keep my optimism strong throughout difficult situations.

Mentorship as a Path for Personal Growth

My life exemplifies the transformative power of mentorship. While facing challenges posed by working in an industry dominated by men, mentors helped me navigate those waters with insight from not just technical expertise or business acumen but also resilience, adaptability, and staying true to one's values.

Starting my dental practice at Williamsburg Center for Dental Health was one of the biggest leaps of faith I ever took. It challenged all that I knew and my ability to mentor others. Over time, as my practice developed, I became an advisor and mentor to my team members, teaching them all aspects of dentistry while simultaneously creating an atmosphere of respect, kindness, and excellence within our clinic environment.

Environment & Mindset—Examining their Interrelations

Environment plays a pivotal role in mentoring. Fostering an encouraging, caring atmosphere at my dental practice is paramount for growth—both for me and those I mentor. Through hard work on both sides, we have succeeded in cultivating an atmosphere in which patients and staff feel supported while operating with positive intentions in an encouraging community—ultimately leading to remarkable achievements!

This philosophy extends to patient care as well. Every interaction I have with patients presents me with an opportunity to mentor, educate, and empower them regarding their oral health needs and well-being. I learned this holistic approach from my mentors and am proud to pass it on to my team and peers daily.

Faith as my Foundation of Mentorship

Faith and mentorship philosophy have always been at the core of my life. Belief in an all-powerful higher power has given me the strength to face my challenges head-on and guide others through their difficulties. Not only am I spiritual in private matters, but my beliefs also guide my decisions and actions across work environments and relationships.

Much like Dr. Wayne Dyer's words about aligning oneself with positive frequencies, faith, like frequency, enables me to keep a positive and hopeful mindset even during challenging times. My role as a mentor requires not only imparting technical knowledge and professional experience; I am also accountable for imparting purposeful, faith-filled enactment to those I mentor.

Mentorship in My Family Life

As the mother of three daughters, I have taken on the additional role of mentor at home. Through hard work, faith, and compassion-instilling parenting philosophies taught to me by my parents, I strive to instill these same qualities in them, too. Balancing my professional responsibilities alongside motherhood has been challenging but has always seemed complementary rather than conflictive.

My daughters have witnessed me establish a successful business venture while managing the challenges associated with professional life and remaining firm in my faith. Through my example, I hope to have taught them what it means to be a leader, mentor, and person of integrity while drawing strength from learning from them through resilience, creativity, determination, and inspiration. Nothing is more important to me than empowering them with these life experiences.

Scaling My Mentorship Beyond My Professional Sphere

My dedication to mentorship extends far beyond the walls of my dental practice. Through mission work in Honduras and El Salvador with Orphan Helpers and volunteer activities at Williamsburg Community Chapel, I've used my talents and resources to make an impactful difference in people's lives. These experiences have reinforced my faith in mentorship's capacity for transformation while revealing new understandings about compassion, humility, and service.

Through these experiences, I have come to appreciate that mentorship should not be seen as hierarchical but relational. My goal as a mentor, whether mentoring young people in Honduras or helping my colleagues achieve their full potential, is always empowerment-based. My approach stems from my faith, which teaches that all individuals possess great value; our purpose here on Earth should always be service and upliftment.

Leaving a Legacy Through Mentorship

Mentorship is not simply a role but represents an invaluable legacy that my mentors have left me. Their impactful influence was immense for my development as an individual, and thus, I am committed to passing that legacy onto future generations through mentorship. Mentorship means living purposefully, guided by faith, and contributing positively to society.

My mentors have helped shape who I am today, and I continue to honor their legacy by mentoring others with equal dedication, compassion, and integrity. For me personally, success should not only be defined in terms of what one achieves for oneself but also by what one helps others accomplish.

Mentorship has been an exciting journey involving faith, leadership, and positive influence. It has guided me through life's many obstacles while molding me into the leader and mother I am today and creating positive change for others around me. Thanks to faith, I found the strength to overcome the barriers while giving those I mentor an environment where they could excel; through mentoring legacy, I hope my words continue inspiring future generations with positivity.

We can change how we perceive things and what we perceive them. As an educator, mentor, and leader, I have witnessed this truth firsthand. I encourage you to accept each step with faith, positivity, and an aim toward serving others in need.

STACEY HALL

About Dr. Stacey Hall: Dr. Stacey Hall, DDS brings her unique outlook on dental care and her personable optimism to the Williamsburg Center for Dental Health. After nine years of solid dental expertise as a dentist in Williamsburg, she then decided in early 2011 to branch out and open her own local practice, Williamsburg Center for Dental Health.

After completing her degrees from Virginia Tech in 1998, Dr. Hall graduated from VCU's MCV School of Dentistry in 2002, receiving her D.D.S. She is a member of the American Academy of Cosmetic Dentistry, Academy of General Dentistry, the American Dental Association, and was awarded member fellowship to the International Congress of Oral Implantology in 2008. Dr. Hall is a scholar with the internationally renowned Dawson Academy.

She is part-time faculty with the Academy, assistant teaching for courses concerning occlusion and rehabilitation of worn dentition. Dr. Hall also leads their ambassador program. Stacey has been blessed with three beautiful daughters, Lanie, Gracie, and Abbie. One attends the University of Tampa, and the other two are very active in high school. She is a loyal Virginia Tech Football fan and enjoys being on the water on her boat, relaxing at her river house, paddle boarding (even with her dog), skiing, Bible study, and missions work.

Author's Website: *www.WilliamsburgDentalHealth.com*

Book Series Website: *www.TheBookOfMentors.com*

STEPH SHINABERY

MENTORSHIP IN AN EVOLVING WORLD

Mentorship has long been essential in my personal and professional lives; yet, as I navigate this journey, I realize its evolution. Where once mentors served solely as sources of advice to their mentees, mentoring is increasingly shifting into dynamic reciprocal relationships that benefit both parties involved.

Looking back over my mentors—Steve, my aunt, and my high school basketball coach—I see they shared qualities like authenticity, vulnerability, and genuine connections, which I consider even more critical given today's rapidly morphing world!

In previous chapters in this series, I have described mentors who saw something special in me but couldn't see for myself, investing their time, energy, and wisdom to facilitate my growth. Over time, however, as my experience deepened, I became acutely aware that mentorship involved guidance, alignment, authenticity, and mutual growth. Therefore, in this chapter of my mentorship journey, I investigate its changing form today and its effect on me.

Mentorship is Focused on Authenticity

One of the defining trends of modern mentorship is an increased emphasis on authenticity. While social media and digital communications may lead to superficial interactions, authentic mentoring provides real and meaningful relationships. Being true to yourself—accepting strengths and weaknesses while encouraging others to do likewise—and inviting all parties involved (mentoring participants and mentors) into fully participatory interactions that encourage mutuality between one person and another is what people value most in mentorship relationships! It takes presence for mentoring relationships!

Dr. Wayne W. Dyer once said, "You only ever stay where you are by your choice alone." I find great comfort in this sentiment and adopt it as my approach to mentorship. Being authentic means recognizing our freedom from society or past experiences that put roles or expectations upon us. Breaking free is the cornerstone of success in mentorship relationships!

My journey to authenticity has not always been easy; at times, expressing myself freely without fearing judgment or rejection was difficult. With mentors' guidance and example as my guideposts, I learned the power of being true to oneself to create impactful mentorship relationships. By being authentic individuals, we create an atmosphere where others feel safe expressing themselves freely without judgment from outside sources. Mutual authenticity forms lasting bonds beyond traditional mentorship relationships.

Acceptance of Mentor-Mentee Align

Modern mentorship has evolved with an increased emphasis on alignment. In the past, mentorship often consisted of authoritarian arrangements wherein experts taught their protegees their craft; modern mentoring seeks to build partnerships based upon shared values, goals, and visions, which helps ensure both professionally and personally beneficial relationships are fostered between mentors and protegees.

My relationship with Steve taught me the power of alignment. Not only was he a professional advice provider, but we also established win-win situations where both parties gained equally from our shared growth over time.

Genius Code Academy highlights the value of mentorship that aligns with one's values and personal journey. Aligning with one's values can create synergies that facilitate growth while expanding horizons for discovery.

Modern Mentorship Takes on its Reciprocal Form

Today's mentorship has undergone significant changes to make it into what it is today. It is no longer an unbalanced trust; instead, it operates like a two-way street where both parties learn, grow, and benefit equally. This mutuality makes mentorship an impactful form of relationship building; exchanging experiences can enrich both sides.

Mentorship has taught me as much from my mentees as it has from me. Their fresh perspectives, creative ideas, and energetic enthusiasm inspired and challenged my thinking about bringing about change! Mutual learning makes mentorship such an enjoyable experience—it's not simply imparting knowledge; mentorship means growing together!

A friend came to me with an outstanding project idea that perfectly aligned with Genius Code Academy values, yet, as I worked together with her, I soon discovered I was learning just as much from her as from me—her enthusiasm and creativity inspired my approach to work more meaningfully and gave me a renewed sense of purpose. This experience reinforced once again that mentorship should be seen as mutually beneficial, with both parties having something valuable to contribute.

Living Authentically: Responsibilities of Mentors

As mentors, we must live lives that reflect who we are. Our mentees rely on us not just for advice but as role models when faced with life's obstacles and difficulties. Being authentic means accepting ourselves even when that may prove challenging. Being open about struggles or vulnerabilities while teaching students that it's okay to make mistakes is a hallmark of authentic mentors.

Dr. Wayne W. Dyer often highlighted the value of living authentically; according to him, by doing so, we can inspire others to follow in our footsteps and embrace authenticity as part of their everyday lives. I take Dr. Wayne W. Dyer's words seriously when mentoring, striving to live authentically while realizing my example can make an immense difference for those within my sphere of influence.

One of the key lessons I have learned as a mentor is that authenticity breeds authenticity. By showing up as authentic versions of ourselves, we create an environment in which others feel safe expressing themselves openly as well, forging stronger ties between students and mentors that exceed traditional mentoring and building stronger bonds of mutual respect, trust, and growth for both parties involved.

Harnessing Vulnerability in Mentorship as a Competitive Edge

Vulnerability is another integral aspect of modern mentorship, although once considered undesirable. Gone are the days when mentors were seen as unwavering figures who always knew all the answers; now, vulnerability is seen as an asset. Creating safe spaces where mentors are willing to show weakness allows mentees the freedom and space they need for personal expression and growth.

As part of my mentorship journey, I've come to recognize that the power of vulnerability is not weakness—instead, it provides a remarkable platform for connection and growth. Sharing struggles and challenges helps mentees see they're not alone on their journey while opening up more about themselves fully, creating deeper bonds of friendship, mutual respect, and greater mutual understanding between us all.

Mentorship to Help Achieve Digital Era Success

Digital innovation has revolutionized how we view mentoring. While traditional face-to-face mentoring remains highly beneficial, digital communications channels now enable new forms of connecting across continents, time zones, and cultural borders thanks to technological innovations like Zoom.

Digital mentorship has enabled me to expand my reach, connecting with individuals who share my values and vision. Thanks to online platforms, I've mentored individuals all around the globe by helping unlock their potential and achieve their goals; this digital approach to mentorship has broadened my scope while broadening my perspective from different experiences and viewpoints.

Digital mentorship presents its own distinct challenges. Forming authentic, meaningful connections may prove more challenging when communication occurs solely via text and video calls, making establishing lasting mentorship relationships in this space challenging. To address these hurdles, I strive to develop intentional interactions between myself and my mentees—through personalized messages, virtual workshops, or one-on-one video sessions—prioritizing authenticity and vulnerability as part of creating powerful digital mentoring relationships that transcend virtual borders.

Next Steps in Mentorship

Mentorship's most rewarding aspects lie in its potential to have an immense ripple effect far beyond any single relationship. When we invest in others, they, in turn, become mentors themselves—spreading the knowledge, wisdom, and support they've received into communities across society, creating growth through empowerment and positive transformation. Mentoring leaves a legacy of growth behind it all.

At Genius Code Academy, I've witnessed this transformation firsthand. Many of my mentees use the tools and insights acquired to assist others on their journeys, truly showing its transformative powers that extend far beyond individual aid to create positive change throughout society! Mentorship truly has incredible transforming potential!

Dr. Wayne W. Dyer once observed, "Our lives are the sum total of choices we've made; as mentors, we wield immense influence over these decisions—not only those our mentees make themselves but also the various actions their choices affect." By living authentically, accepting vulnerability, and cultivating alignment, we can leave behind an impactful legacy of mentorship to empower future generations.

Continue the Mentorship Revolution

As my mentorship journey unfolds, I am more committed than ever to embracing modern mentorship principles and revolution. Mentorship goes well beyond simply offering advice: it requires building authentic connections between mentors and mentees, encouraging mutual growth, and leaving an indelible mark on society overall. Mentorship allows us to live our truth while helping empower others on their path toward empowerment.

Dr. Wayne W. Dyer notes: "Loneliness can only exist if one finds comfort with those they spend their alone time with. Our responsibility as mentors lies with helping individuals discover who they truly are so they may live lives filled with purpose, passion and fulfillment—this revolution of mentorship that's changing lives one authentic connection at a time!"

Our Journey Begins Once More

Mentorship is not an endpoint but a journey toward continuous personal and professional development. Mentors journey alongside their mentees on this path together, providing support during highs and lows, successes or challenges encountered along the way, and moments of clarity or confusion experienced along this journey. A journey such as this requires openness, curiosity, and dedication toward our own development and those we mentor.

As I've explored mentorship further, I have come to recognize its greatest effectiveness when we show up fully, authentically, and vulnerable. Acknowledging our imperfections and sharing stories that ring true for others—creating space where everyone feels seen, heard, and valued. True transformation can happen when relationships go beyond superficial surface levels to inspire people to discover their inner power and take steps toward realizing it.

Mentorship is about passing on what we learn to others, leaving an impactful legacy for communities, industries, and societies as a whole.

Dr. Wayne W. Dyer encourages me to enjoy each step along my mentorship journey, just like dancing requires enjoying each step along its path—not as an endpoint but as an enjoyable process of growth, connection, and mutual empowerment for both parties involved.

I encourage you to embrace the mentorship revolution in your own life. Seek mentors whose values and vision align with yours or become mentors yourself for others. Live authentically while giving freely; together, we can transform mentorship into a powerful force for positive change!

STEPH SHINABERY

About Steph Shinabery: Steph Shinabery is The World's Best Possibility Coach, and a Nurse Anesthesiologist, Artist, Speaker, and the Founder of GENIUS CODE ACADEMY.

After spending much of her life in a career that lacked the inspiration and fulfillment she knew was available to her, she began a journey to answer the question: "What is it I truly desire?"

Her journey led to the creation of the Genius Identity Code™, a process for unlocking your gift, purpose and path, and helping people see, believe and execute their unique genius to achieve miraculous outcomes.

Steph works with creative experts, entrepreneurs and coaches to help them embrace their authenticity and create a life that gets them excited to jump out of bed every day!

You can find her talk, "Wake Up Your Genius Machine," on Amazon Prime Video's *Speak Up: Empower Your Ideas, Season 4.*

Author's Website: *www.StephShinabery.com* &
www.GeniusCodeAcademy.com

Book Series Website: *www.TheBookOfMentors.com*

TAYLOR L. COLE

WHAT'S WEIGHING DOWN YOUR MENTORSHIP JOURNEY?

My church hosted a weekend leadership summit for about 600 people who lead small groups, volunteer teams, community projects, and other areas of our church's ministry. After a time of worship and reflection, the senior staff shared with us their definition of a leader. While we've all heard various definitions of leaders and have personal examples of leaders in our lives, my church wanted to get everyone on the same page and align our understanding with the direction we see our church heading.

Before they shared this definition, my mind immediately went to standard definitions of a leader, such as the Oxford Dictionary's definition, which describes a leader as "the person who leads or commands a group, organization, or country." However, leadership extends beyond merely commanding or directing others.

Another powerful definition views a leader as someone who empowers others to realize their potential and achieve collective goals. This perspective emphasizes that leadership is not just about authority or control, but about influence, inspiration, and fostering an environment where everyone can contribute meaningfully. Leaders are those who cultivate trust, build relationships, and encourage growth—not just within the group they lead, but also in each individual's personal journey.

In the context of spiritual mentoring, this means guiding others in their faith journey, offering wisdom, establishing accountability, supporting their spiritual growth, and working together to fulfill a mission.

In *The Book of Mentors*, honoring one of the Legacy Legends, Brian Tracy, I contrasted discipleship and mentorship. A disciple is a student, learner, or follower who is becoming like the one they are following for the sake of others. A disciple is trained to become like their teacher with a heart of generosity.

My church shared the definition of a leader: "A leader is a disciple of Jesus who takes responsibility to create kingdom culture and make disciples while accomplishing a specific task." To effectively take on this responsibility and cultivate a fruitful culture, you often need to let go of anything that's holding you back.

When I think about discipleship and the disciples in the Bible, I'm reminded of the profound sacrifices they made to follow Jesus. These individuals gave up everything they knew and cherished to walk in His footsteps. Take Matthew, for example—once a tax collector, he abandoned his lucrative occupation to follow Jesus. Similarly, Peter and Andrew, brothers who made their living as fishermen, left behind their nets and boats to answer Jesus' call. Other disciples left behind family, friends, and the familiar comforts of their previous lives. They relinquished their worldly possessions and livelihoods to become dedicated followers and mentees of Jesus.

But their sacrifices weren't just material. Beyond giving up their tangible belongings, the disciples also faced the challenge of releasing emotional burdens. They had to learn to let go of deep-seated feelings such as resentment and fear, laying these at Jesus' feet. Discipleship required them to trust Jesus not only with their futures but also with their pasts, surrendering the emotional weights they had carried for so long.

In following Jesus, they embraced a new way of life—one that required both external and internal transformation. The journey of discipleship is not just about what they left behind in the physical world, but also about the inner healing and freedom they found in Christ.

In Luke 9:3, Jesus gave a powerful yet surprising instruction to His disciples: "Take nothing for your journey—no walking stick, no traveler's bag, no food, money, or even a change of clothes." This directive wasn't just about traveling light physically; it also had spiritual implications.

As leaders who are both mentoring others and being mentored ourselves, we must consider what burdens we're carrying in our own traveler's bag. When we take the time to unpack it, we often find that our traveler's bag is weighed down with issues deeply rooted in pride and fear. These roots can manifest as a heavy load of unforgiveness—lingering hurts from the past, disappointments, injustices, betrayals, and wrongs that have left lasting marks on our hearts.

Unpacking Unforgiveness in Leadership

Unforgiveness is more than just holding onto past wrongs—it's a burden that can significantly impact our leadership and personal growth. Forgiveness is essential, but it's important to understand what it truly means. Forgiving doesn't imply that what happened to us was acceptable, nor does it erase or minimize the pain we've experienced.

Instead, forgiveness is about releasing our right to seek retribution or repayment for the wrongs done to us. It's a conscious choice to let go of the bitterness and resentment that can otherwise weigh us down and prevent us from moving forward.

The implications of unforgiveness in leadership are heavy. Practically speaking, unforgiveness can manifest in various ways:

Holding onto Grudges: When we cling to past grievances whether with colleagues, competitors, or even ourselves—we allow resentment to fester. This lingering negativity can cloud our judgment and create unnecessary tension, making it difficult to form the productive relationships that are essential for career and personal growth. A leader burdened by grudges may find themselves reacting defensively, misinterpreting others' intentions, or avoiding certain people altogether.

Over time, this can erode trust and create a toxic environment where cooperation and collaboration are stifled.

Leaders are called to embody the principles of grace and forgiveness, setting an example for others to follow. However, when leaders hold onto grudges, it becomes challenging to foster a community of love and acceptance. The very relationships that should be nurtured can become strained, and unity can be compromised.

Impeding Collaboration: Unforgiveness also creates barriers to effective collaboration. For example, if a leader harbors unresolved anger or distrust toward a teammate or colleague, it becomes challenging to work together, share ideas, or support one another's success. These barriers can hinder individual progress and the overall success of the team. Collaboration requires a foundation of trust and mutual respect. When unforgiveness is present, it's like a wall that separates team members, preventing them from fully engaging with one another.

This is particularly true in leadership settings where collaboration is key to achieving common goals. Whether in the workplace, in ministry, or in personal relationships, unresolved issues can prevent the free flow of ideas and stifle the creative problem-solving process. Leaders who are unable to forgive may find themselves isolated, unable to effectively lead and mentor their teams or foster the kind of innovation that drives progress.

Stifling Creativity & Innovation: The mental energy consumed by unforgiveness can stifle creativity and innovation. When a leader is preoccupied with past wrongs, it's harder to think clearly, take risks, and explore new ideas. This fixation can limit their ability to mentor with vision and drive transformational change, because their focus remains on the past rather than on future possibilities. Creativity thrives in environments where people feel safe to take risks and express themselves freely. When unforgiveness clouds a leader's mind, it can create an atmosphere of fear and caution, where new ideas are snuffed out before they can even be explored.

What's more, unforgiveness can lead to a fixed mindset, where leaders become more focused on protecting themselves from further harm rather than pursuing growth and new opportunities. This mindset can limit a mentor's ability to inspire and motivate others as they become more concerned with maintaining control rather than with pushing boundaries and driving change.

Undermining Leadership Presence: Leaders who struggle with unforgiveness may come across as rigid, unapproachable, or overly critical. This demeanor can erode trust and respect within their teams, making it harder to inspire and motivate others. A lack of forgiveness can also prevent leaders from showing vulnerability or empathy—traits that are essential for building strong, effective teams and in fostering meaningful mentor/mentee relationships. Leadership presence is not just about being authoritative; it's about being relatable and compassionate.

When leaders hold onto unforgiveness, they may find it difficult to connect with others on a deeper level. They may appear distant or unapproachable, which can create a barrier between them and their team members. This can lead to a breakdown in communication and a lack of trust, both of which are essential for effective leadership. Without trust and open communication, it becomes challenging to inspire and lead others toward a common goal.

Blocking Personal Growth: Finally, unforgiveness often ties leaders to past hurts and mistakes, preventing them from moving forward. This can foster a fixed mindset, where the focus shifts from growth and new opportunities to self-protection and avoidance of further harm. When you find yourself bringing up past hurts, it's crucial to recognize the weight they add and to remember to release them, allowing for personal and professional growth.

In the context of discipleship, personal growth is not just about developing new skills or acquiring knowledge; it's about spiritual growth and becoming more like Christ. Unforgiveness can be a significant hindrance to this process. It can keep us stuck in a cycle of negativity and bitterness, preventing us from experiencing the fullness of life that God has for us. By holding onto past hurts, we limit our ability to grow in our faith and in our relationships with others.

Releasing Unforgiveness: A Path to Freedom

To truly lead, we must first be willing to let go of what's holding us back. This includes the emotional and spiritual burdens we carry in our "traveler's bag." Just as Jesus instructed His disciples to take nothing unnecessary on their journey, we, too, are called to release these burdens, allowing us to lead with a heart that is free and open, fully trusting in God's provision and guidance along the way.

As Wayne Dyer once said, "You cannot always control what goes on outside. But you can always control what goes on inside." This reminds us that the journey of leadership and discipleship is as much about managing our inner world as it is about guiding others. When we address these burdens of unforgiveness, rooted in pride and fear, we can lighten our load and lead with greater clarity, creativity, and compassion.

This journey of letting go is not always easy, but it is essential for effective leadership. It requires us to confront the pain and hurt we've experienced while embracing opportunities to learn as we grow with those we lead and mentor.

Are you ready to take your next steps?

1. What burdens are you carrying in your "traveler's bag" that might be holding you back from fully stepping into your role as a leader or mentor?

2. Is there any unforgiveness, rooted in pride or fear, that you need to release in order to grow as a leader and mentor?

3. How can you actively cultivate trust, build stronger relationships, and encourage growth in those you are mentoring or leading?

4. In what ways can you rely more on God's provision and guidance as you let go of past hurts and embrace your journey of leadership?

5. What practical steps can you take this week to mentor someone in their spiritual journey, and offer support and encouragement in their faith?

TLC

TAYLOR L. COLE

About Taylor L. Cole: Taylor L. Cole is a seasoned professional dedicated to helping meaningful brands capture the attention they deserve. With a career spanning over 14 years, Taylor has honed her skills in Communications, PR, and social media, working with Fortune 500 companies, multi-national corporations, and startups across various industries including travel, tech, healthcare, and consumer products. Starting her journey in the world of television while still in high school, Taylor quickly made her mark, producing her first major show as an undergraduate at Southern Methodist University. She has since taken on leadership roles in communications and public relations at renowned companies such as Kimberly Clark, Hotels.com, Expedia, and Sabre.

As a guide for brands and leaders, Taylor specializes in crafting effective messaging and on-camera strategies, featuring her clients on quality, international TV programs and podcasts. She is the executive producer and host of *The Focus* and *Speak Up* on Amazon Prime Video, as well as the travel TV show *Hotel Hunt*, where she explores stunning destinations and uncovers unique accommodations. Her latest project is *Workable Faith*, a show where she engages with business leaders about integrating faith into the marketplace.

Taylor is also a dedicated community member, serving on various non-profit boards, business leadership groups, and actively participating in her church. Her involvement includes roles with the American Diabetes Association, Fellowship Power Lunch, Truth at Work, Valley Creek Church, and SMU.

Author's Website: *www.TVWithTLC.com*

Book Series Website: *www.TheBookOfMentors.com*

VIKKI ROOD

THE GIFT OF GIVING BACK

In the garden of life, the most beautiful flowers bloom under the care of a dedicated gardener. I've had the privilege of nurturing many such blossoms, sharing the water and sunlight that was so generously given to me. This journey of mentoring is not just a path I chose; it chose me, wrapping its vines around my heart and teaching me the essence of giving, inspiring, and creating alongside those who are still finding their footing in this vast garden.

When I rewind to my childhood, I remember being eight years old, the elder sibling to twin brothers and a baby sister. Inevitably, I slipped into the role of a mentor. I was the one showing them the ropes—uncovering cool things, orchestrating games, eliciting laughter, and, often, playing the entertainer. This early experience sparked a lifelong fascination with people—understanding our motives, our actions, and how to create an environment where everyone feels valued and deserving of attention. The question that often danced in my mind was: How can we navigate life in a way that's both smooth and enjoyable?

Life, as we know, isn't always a straight path. It comes with its fair share of bumps, rainy days, and moments shrouded in fog. Through these times, I've discovered a powerful way to weather the storm—my chosen family. These are the people who truly know me, love me, and, importantly, aren't afraid to tell me the truth. Whether it's a piece of food stuck in my teeth or if I'm being overly critical of myself, they're there to offer a reality check. They remind me of the power in choice—the ability to steer my life in a different direction when the current one isn't serving me.

Sharing What Was So Freely Given to Me

My journey into mentoring began on a day painted with the ordinary brush of routine. It wasn't marked by any particular sign or a dramatic turn of events. Instead, it was the realization that the wisdom, love, and support generously showered upon me by mentors of my own were gifts too precious to keep to myself. They were seeds meant to be sown into the lives of others, not treasures to be hoarded.

In every shared experience, every piece of advice given, and every moment of silence filled with understanding, I was passing on a legacy. This legacy was not built on monumental achievements or groundbreaking discoveries, but on simple acts of kindness, moments of vulnerability, and the courage to be genuinely oneself. It was about showing up, day after day, ready to give without the expectation of receiving.

Inspiring Others to Live in Their Authenticity

In the glossy pages of magazines and the curated perfection of social media feeds, it's easy to lose oneself in the pursuit of looking good. The world often feels like a race, where the finish line is adorned with the trappings of success and approval. Yet, in this relentless chase, the essence of who we are begins to blur.

As a mentor, one of my greatest missions is to inspire my mentees to embrace their authentic selves; to remind them that their worth is not tied to the applause of the crowd but resides in the quiet assurance of their uniqueness. Authenticity is the key that unlocks the doors to genuine happiness and fulfillment, and mentoring offers a platform to share this truth.

I've seen the transformative power of authenticity in action. It begins with a tentative step—a shared secret, a confessed dream, or a whispered fear. These moments of openness are like rays of sunlight breaking through the clouds, illuminating the path to self-discovery. By living authentically, I not only guide my mentees toward their own light but also reaffirm my commitment to my true self.

Allowing the Mentees Space to Make Decisions & Be Creative

True growth occurs in the spaces where we are free to explore, make mistakes, and find our own way. As a mentor, my role is not to dictate every step but to provide a safe and nurturing environment where creativity and decision-making flourish. It's about giving my mentees the room to spread their wings, knowing that the flight might be wobbly at first, but trusting in their ability to soar.

This approach requires letting go of control and embracing trust. It's about believing in the potential of my mentees, even when they struggle to see it themselves. Each decision they make, whether it leads to success or serves as a valuable lesson, is a step toward their independence and self-assurance.

The beauty of allowing creative freedom is in the unexpected outcomes. Creativity knows no bounds, and when mentees are empowered to think outside the box, they often surpass their own expectations. These moments of triumph are not just victories for the mentees but shared celebrations that reinforce the value of our interconnectedness.

The Interconnectedness that Matters

In a world that celebrates individualism, the concept of interconnectedness seems almost revolutionary. Yet, it is in our very nature to seek connection, to find solace in the presence of those who understand and share our journey. Mentoring, at its core, is an embodiment of this interconnectedness. It's a reminder that we are not islands, but part of a vast, intricate network of lives touching lives.

The mentor-mentee relationship is a beautiful illustration of this principle. It's a partnership that acknowledges the value of every individual's journey while recognizing that our paths are interwoven. We used to take care of each other in communities where every person's role was acknowledged, and through mentoring, we can recapture this sense of belonging and purpose.

This interconnectedness extends beyond the immediate relationships to influence the broader community. As mentees grow into their potential and start to share their own gifts, the ripple effect is profound. They become mentors in their own right, perpetuating the cycle of giving, inspiring, and creating. This chain reaction is a testament to the enduring power of our connections, proving that when we uplift one another, the entire community thrives.

Mentoring is more than just a role; it's a journey of mutual growth, discovery, and transformation. It's about sharing the wisdom that was so freely given to me, inspiring others to live authentically, and allowing them the space to discover for themselves what their truth is!

VIKKI ROOD

About Vikki Rood: Vikki Rood is a passionate advocate for joyful living, a seasoned empowerment coach, and a published author dedicated to helping individuals uncover their authentic selves and live lives filled with purpose, empowerment, and boundless joy. Vikki invites you to join her on a journey of self-discovery, empowerment, and joy.

Through coaching, workshops, and a thriving community, she'll help you uncover your authentic self, embrace your unique path, and find fulfillment in every facet of your life.

Author's Website: *www.VikkiRoodCoaching.com*

Book Series Website: *www.TheBookOfMentors.com*

HONORING DR. WAYNE DYER

"HEAVEN ON EARTH IS A CHOICE YOU MUST MAKE, NOT A PLACE YOU MUST FIND."

~ DR. WAYNE DYER

WILLIAM BLAKE

REAL LEADERSHIP—REAL IMPACT

"Truly inspiring leaders get results by their own example: They encourage others to be responsible and do the right thing... they create space for others to be inspired and to achieve their own greatness."
~ **Dr. Wayne Dyer**

We all have a desire for something: money, fame, love, family, a certain title, trophy, or various other things. "I want what I want, and I want it now!" seems to be the mantra in society. And I don't think that's entirely bad. But what separates the ones who get it from the ones who just dream about it? Both the poor and the rich want to be wealthy, but only one is. What is that difference?

When I first started networking and masterminding, I was hooked on information. I was a novice at best when it came to my knowledge. I was so hungry to learn that I carried a notebook with me all the time—to church, events, reunions, virtual trainings. Everywhere I went, I had a notebook.

After doing this for several years, I noticed I was the only one doing it. At all the events, I was the only one writing ideas down. Other people who I found impressive didn't have anything, just them and their business cards. Having my notebook didn't feel wrong; it helped me a lot. But since no one else did it, I thought that maybe I was the uninformed one. I started to leave my notebook on my nightstand at home. I would still write notes down every night, but the judgment I thought others were giving stopped me from bringing it to meetings.

A few months after stopping, I had a unique experience. I was talking with a group of wantrepreneurs at a networking event, all of us standing there trying to impress each other with things we were going to get done. Then I felt a tap on my shoulder. I looked around and found someone I'd met multiple times during these events. We shook hands and started talking about how life was going. About five minutes in, he looked me up and down and asked, "Where's your notebook?" I was hoping no one had noticed. I told him I kept it at home since it seemed the best people didn't write things down.

He taught me an important lesson that day. "You do what works for you, and you'll make it further than anyone else in this room," he said. He continued to explain that the highest performers write things down all the time. People like Tony Robbins and Brian Tracy always advocate for writing things down. Forbes and Harvard have published research articles about the advantages of putting pen to paper. Before he left, he told me to get that notebook and start writing in it again. "People try to impress others all the time, but it's the ones who are truly impressive by what they've done who say, 'Do what works for you.'" After that, I went home, grabbed my notebook, and to this day, you will always see me carrying a notebook around.

This lesson got me thinking about who people are versus who people portray themselves to be, and the gap in-between. What sets the rich apart from the poor is the action and experience they have. I'm sure you've met someone who dreams big but has never taken action. Compare that person to someone who has already done it—two different people. Like the man who told me to be myself at events, I find that the experienced are the ones who are considered *mentor leaders*.

What is a Mentor Leader?

Mentor leaders are people who guide and support others by sharing their knowledge and experiences. They foster growth and build trusting relationships with those they meet. They lead their lives with authenticity, purpose, and a commitment to serve others. Interestingly, mentor leaders can be any age. It's not about the age as much as the miles they've traveled. One of my mentors is a ten-year-old crushing it in the non-profit world. Another is a ninety-eight-year-old gentleman living an extravagant life with his spouse, kids, and grandkids.

While at college working on my degree, I came a few minutes early to a business class. There was a new guy sitting in the seat I usually sat in, so I sat next to it and started up a conversation. We had a great chat about work, college life, and our goals. He seemed like a very interesting college student. Class started, and after the announcement items, the professor pointed to the guy next to me and introduced him as a guest speaker. He stood up, and we found out he was one of the top ecommerce salesmen in the nation. I sat in awe that someone who seemed like a normal college student was someone so accomplished. It's about the life they've experienced more than the years they've been alive.

Like with age, this encounter highlighted an important aspect of leadership: authenticity. Authentic leaders don't necessarily stand out at first glance because they don't feel the need to show off their accomplishments. Instead, their true value and influence become evident through their genuine interactions and the respect they command from those who know them well. This experience got me thinking more about how authentic leaders operate and why their authenticity is such a powerful trait.

The Importance of Authenticity

One of the most profound qualities that mentor leaders exhibit is authenticity. Authenticity in leadership is about being genuine, transparent, and true to one's values and beliefs. Mentor leaders do not wear masks or pretend to be someone they are not; instead, they embrace their true selves and encourage others to do the same. This real approach creates an environment of trust and respect, which is essential for any mentorship relationship to succeed.

Consider my experience with the notebook. Early in my journey, I was self-conscious about carrying a notebook everywhere I went, fearing judgment from others. However, when a seasoned networker encouraged me to continue with my habit because it worked for me, I learned a crucial lesson about authenticity. This advice wasn't just about the practicality of taking notes; it was about the importance of staying true to myself despite external pressures. Authentic mentor leaders recognize that each person's unique approach is valuable and should be embraced.

Building Trust Through Transparency

Authenticity also involves transparency. Mentor leaders are open about their successes and their failures. They do not shy away from discussing the mistakes they've made or the challenges they've faced. This level of honesty builds trust because people can see that their mentors are not infallible but are instead individuals who have learned and grown from their experiences.

For instance, one of my mentors, a successful entrepreneur, once shared with me his early business failures. Rather than diminishing his credibility, this transparency made his advice more impactful. It showed me that setbacks are part of the journey, and that perseverance is key. His willingness to be open about his struggles provided me with a more realistic and encouraging perspective on my own challenges.

Live the Life that Works for You

Reflecting on my journey and the lessons I've learned from mentor leaders, it's clear that authenticity is a cornerstone of effective leadership. Mentor leaders who are genuine, transparent, and true to their values create a powerful ripple effect, inspiring trust and fostering an environment where real growth can occur.

By embracing authenticity, we not only stay true to ourselves but also encourage others to do the same. This authenticity builds stronger, more trusting relationships and provides a solid foundation for personal and professional development. As you seek out mentor leaders and strive to become one yourself, remember that the power of authenticity cannot be overstated. It is through being genuine and transparent that we can truly lead, inspire, and make a lasting impact.

In your journey, hold onto what makes you unique and never shy away from being your true self. The path to success is not about conforming to others' expectations but about embracing your authentic self and finding mentors who do the same. Authenticity is not just a quality of great leaders; it is the essence of leadership itself.

WILLIAM BLAKE

About William Blake: William is a speaker and motivator. He focuses on the skill sets of learning, listening, and observing to help people access new avenues of success and solutions. What might seem like regular everyday skills that most overlook, William teaches people how to find creative ways of accessing those skills.

William Blake is a stalwart professional in the world of organization, strategy, and methods. Being diagnosed with Dyslexia at a young age and struggling with reading and speaking, William is an example that through perseverance, any challenge can become a superpower.

William spearheads a dynamic coaching and speaking venture, empowering dyslexics to harness their unique strengths and embrace a world of boundless possibilities. He is also one of the chapter team leaders and corporate associates at Champion Circle Professional Association founded by Jon Kovach Jr.

From speaking to youth to being a camp counselor at Idaho Diabetes Youth Programs, William loves volunteering and helping children and teens believe in themselves and their unlimited potential. And of most importance to William is his love for his family. With his wife, he is dedicated to raising his daughters in a world of greatness, happiness, and unlimited belief.

Author's website: *www.WilliamBlakeLight.com*

Book Series Website: *www.TheBookOfMentors.com*

Habitude Warrior Mastermind

Join a team of
AWESOME
Entrepreneurs, Coaches, Business Owners, and Leaders to support you in your journey of success!

Be one of my personal guests for a session!
www.MastermindGuestPass.com

HABITUDE WARRIOR & INTEGRITY PUBLISHING EDITORIAL TEAM

Habitude Warrior International and Integrity Publishing take great pride in our editorial team who put their sweat, tears, and heart into each and every project and national bestseller! Thank you team!

JON KOVACH JR.
Team Manager

Jon Kovach Jr. strives to assist every author and every team member in the process of self-development for ultimate success.

PAT MINTON
VP of Operations

Pat Minton has been with the Habitude Warrior International team for over 20 years getting her start with Brian Tracy & Erik Swanson.

JILLIAN KOVACH
Editorial Manager

Jillian is a vital team member of Habitude Warrior & Integrity Publishing bringing her expertise managing our Editorial Department.

FATIMA HURD
Editorial Team & Photographer

Fatima is our Professional Photographer for Habitude Warrior as well as one of our members on the Proofing Department team.

LAUREN COBB
Editorial Team Member

Lauren Cobb is part of our Proofing Department for Habitude Warrior & Integrity Publishing as well as one of our authors.

To inquire about joining our team please send us an email to Team@HabitudeWarrior.com

HONORING DR. WAYNE DYER